Top Global Companies

Companies

J^{IN}APAN

Akira Ishikawa

Tai Nejo

World Scientific

NEW JERSEY · LONDON · SINGAPORE · SHANGHAI · HONG KONG · TAIPEI · CHENNAI

Published by

World Scientific Publishing Co. Pte. Ltd.

5 Toh Tuck Link, Singapore 596224

USA office: Suite 202, 1060 Main Street, River Edge, NJ 07661

UK office: 57 Shelton Street, Covent Garden, London WC2H 9HE

British Library Cataloguing-in-Publication Data
A catalogue record for this book is available from the British Library.

TOP GLOBAL COMPANIES IN JAPAN

This English edition published in 2004 is a translation of the Japanese edition NIHON NO NAKANO SEKAIICHIKIGYO, published in Japan in 1999 by The SANNO Institute of Management Publications Department.

ISBN 981-238-684-X

Printed in Singapore by World Scientific Printers (S) Pte Ltd

Preface

Despite the largest economic-stimulus packages ever initiated in rapid succession, Japan's economy has shown no sign of recovery. The *World Economy Forecast* published by the IMF (International Monetary Fund) at the end of 1998 predicted that Japan's net annual economic growth rate for 1999 would be minus 0.5%, which makes Japan the only country showing negative growth among the seven developed countries in the world. Does this indicate the continued decline of Japan's economy?

What symbolizes the current economical situation in Japan is the decline of large corporations. For example, both Yamaichi Security and Hokkaido Takushoku Bank have been dissolved. The Long-Term Credit Bank of Japan and Nippon Credit Bank have gone under as well. Large conglomerates such as Hitachi, Toshiba and Mitsubishi Electric, which have long represented Japanese industry, have also declined. Their preoccupation with the expansion of their organization at the expense of efficiency has become an apparent weakness.

Until the 1980s, being big was an asset. In the past ten years, however, the environment surrounding corporations has completely changed. The market has become increasingly fast-paced, diversified and specialized. Large corporations devoid of individuality and imagination now find themselves incapable of meeting the needs of the new market. Their slowness in decision-making has also proven detrimental. Large corporations that are simply a collection of noncompetitive businesses face the question of their very survival. Thus, being big has become a liability.

On the other hand, it is said that reformation is born on a frontier. In the middle of the current protracted recession, new powers have gathered strength to face the 21st century. Using their speed and specialty as leverage, a group of specialized medium-sized companies are rising. They have not yet been in the spotlight, but they have a top market share worldwide in their specialized fields. We call them *Top Global Companies* in this book.

How have they climbed to the top of the global market while many of the large companies have fallen into a slump? We will answer this question by shedding light on their strategies and organization for high earnings, the secret of "producing something from nothing" and "enabling the lesser to win against the greater".

Incidentally, what are the principles to follow, if any, to become a No. 1 in the world market? We will seek to answer this question by analyzing eighteen *Top Global Companies*.

Japanese companies are strenuously looking for new management styles in this era of great competition. According to the "Questionnaire to 100 Presidents of Companies", which was conducted by the Nihon Keizai Shimbun in April 1998, 70% of the presidents who responded said that "specialized companies focused on specific niches will manifest their strength in the new era". They recognized the typical management style of *Top Global Companies* as a model for the 21st century.

There are still many corporate leaders who blame external factors such as politics and foreign exchange fluctuation for their companies' poor performance. They have forgotten that it is companies and the individuals within them that have to be energized for a vibrant economy. They should learn from the self-reliant effort and entrepreneurship of *Top Global Companies*. It is the authors' wish that this book may convey their wisdom and energy to sustain its readers through this era of globalization.

Tokyo
March 1999

Akira Ishikawa
Tai Nejo

Contents

Chapter One

Obscure Top Global Companies in Japan

I. Decline of Large Corporations in Japan

Entering the 21st century has failed to energize corporate Japan. Especially conspicuous is the decline of large corporations that led the global market in the 1980s. Once representing "strong companies", large manufacturing conglomerates such as Nissan Motor, Mitsubishi Motors, Hitachi, and Toshiba have seen their performance deteriorate. With no regard for appearances, they have grappled with restructuring by withdrawing from unprofitable operations, reducing headcount, or spinning off business units into stand-alone companies.

The situation is worse with financial institutions plagued by bad loans. Leading banks are not exceptions; Hokkaido Takushoku Bank, the Long-Term Credit Bank of Japan, and Nippon Credit Bank have gone under. Construction companies have yet to recover from the collapse of the bubble economy (1990), and many have been eliminated by natural selection.

The decline of the Japanese economy is also confirmed by statistics. IMD, an influential business school in Switzerland, publishes every year the rankings of countries in international competitiveness. What is measured is the environment which helps companies sustain competitiveness. In 1998, Japan slipped from the No. 1 position it had enjoyed since 1993 to No. 18. It was ranked below other Asian countries such as

Singapore and Hong Kong. Watching the decline of Japan's international competitiveness is unbearable.

How do we account for this decline? Large corporations led the Japanese economy after the Second World War. They used to run numerous businesses to avoid risks for their entire organization. Changes in the external environment, however, transformed their strength into weakness. Technological innovation accelerated and the lifecycle of goods shortened. Customers' needs drastically changed and diversified.

"Speedy" and "diverse" markets permitted specialized manufacturers to exercise their strength. They overwhelmed large corporations, thereby increasing their market shares. The "supermarket-style management" of a mere collection of unprofitable businesses was then bogged down, causing large corporations to struggle with poor performance. "Speed" or "specialization" is hard to create within a giant organization. Thus, large corporations are being pressed for organizational reform as well.

Chart 1-1   IMD International Competitiveness Ranking of Japan

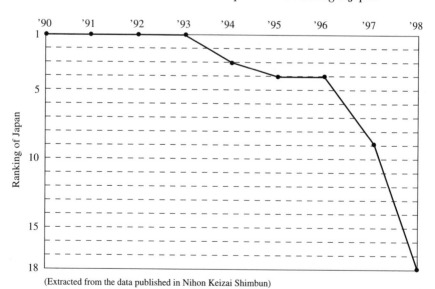

(Extracted from the data published in Nihon Keizai Shimbun)

Chart 1-2   Decline of Large Corporations

(Sales in million yen; dividends in yen)

	Fiscal period	Sales	Operating income	Ordinary income	Net income	Dividend
Hitachi	4/'98–9/'98 (act.)	1,798,906	▲55,806	▲69,244	▲124,664	0
	4/'97–3/'98 (act.)	4,078,030	46,784	17,220	10,236	11
	4/'98–3/'99 (est.)	3,720,000	▲80,000	▲100,000	▲260,000	0~11
Toshiba Corp.	4/'98–9/'98 (act.)	1,599,946	4,262	▲6,401	▲6,401	3
	4/'97–3/'98 (act.)	3,699,968	47,194	38,601	33,046	10
	4/'98–3/'99 (est.)	3,500,000	40,000	15,000	12,000	6~10
Mitsubishi Electric	4/'98–9/'98 (act.)	1,306,113	11,507	4,342	2,479	0
	4/'97–3/'98 (act.)	2,811,510	21,632	4,225	▲33,853	4
	4/'98–3/'99 (est.)	2,800,000	40,000	30,000	20,000	0~4
Nissan Motor	4/'98–9/'98 (act.)	1,638,584	20,607	28,844	▲32,548	0
	4/'97–3/'98 (act.)	3,546,126	85,626	57,707	16,548	10
	4/'98–3/'99 (est.)	3,400,000	50,000	70,000	▲45,000	5
Mitsubishi Motors	4/'98–9/'98 (act.)	1,106,280	▲15,145	▲18,299	▲28,637	0
	4/'97–3/'98 (act.)	2,500,614	▲15,512	▲22,157	▲25,656	3.5
	4/'98–3/'99 (est.)	2,300,000	▲9,000	▲20,000	▲34,000	0

(Source: Toyo Keizai, 12 December 1998, p. 16)

II. High-Spirited Medium-Sized Companies Competing in the World Market

Looking askance at the decline of large corporations, a number of medium-sized companies in Japan are flourishing in the world market. They are specialized manufacturers which have captured global markets in their own niches using "speed" and "specialization" as leverage. They are not household names, but are powerful companies whose products enjoy top shares in global markets. The authors call these medium-sized

companies *Top Global Companies* which are not limited to the manufacturers of products that command top shares in global markets.
Take a look at Seven-Eleven Japan, Yamato Transport, and Secom, for
example. They created their own new businesses. Their creations, that
is, convenience stores, door-to-door parcel delivery service, and a
centralized security system, did not exist in Japan 30 years ago, but have
become integral parts of our contemporary life. Although their main

Chart 1-3   Specialized Manufacturers and Their Products Having a
Top Worldwide Market Share

Manufacturers	Products	Worldwide Market Share[1]
Murata Manufacturing	Ceramic filters	80%
Nidec	HDD spindle motors	70%
Advantest	Memory testers	60%
Rohm	Print heads for facsimile machines	34%
Nakashima Propeller	Marine propellers	40%
Keyence	[2]	[2]
Mabuchi Motor	Small DC motors	50%
Minebea	HDD pivot assemblies	70%
Tokyo Electron	Diffusion furnaces, CVD equipment	48%
Yupo Corporation	Synthetic paper	80%
Disco	Grinding and cutting machines for semiconductors	70%
Horiba	Engine emission analyzers	80%
Canon Kasei	Toner cartridges for laser beam printers	70%
Denso	Car air-conditioners	20%
Nippon Electric Glass	Cathode-ray tube glass	30%

Notes:
[1]Including estimates
[2]No data available
(Extracted from references used in the book)

battle fields are domestic markets, the excellent management know-how they have established is to set "global standards". They therefore also deserve to be called *Top Global Companies*.

Prominent characteristics of a "top global company" are its high profit-earning capacity and growth rate. In comparison with 2.82% average ROE (Return on Equity) of the listed companies in fiscal 1997 (Nikkei Management Index, Fall 1998), *Top Global Companies* have achieved considerably higher returns, with Advantest's 19.9% ROE at the top. They have achieved high capital efficiency and are structured to yield high profit. Except for Yamato Transport, Disco, and Nippon Electric Glass, they are all young enterprises founded after the Second World War. Keyence, Seven-Eleven Japan, and Nidec, for example, are less than 30 years old considering their phenomenal growth rates.

The financial data of *Top Global Companies* are characterized by hockey-stick growth, and in general, the younger they are, the higher their earning power. This trend becomes more apparent when we compare them with integrated electronics manufacturers such as NEC, Hitachi, and Toshiba.

III. Six Strategic Patterns of *Top Global Companies*

Top Global Companies have strong personalities, and therefore each of their strategies is unique. This does not mean that the strategies of *Top Global Companies* have nothing in common.

"Six strategic patterns" emerge out of the analysis of their strategies. The basic strategy of a medium-sized company is to specialize in a niche and concentrate its management resource on that niche. Companies that specialize in niches can be classified into three types in terms of their strategic emphases — speed, customizing, and globalizing. In addition, they may pursue one of three more strategic patterns, that is, creating competitive edge with unique technology developed for the first time in the world, growing in close contact with a parent company, or creating new business.

Chart 1-4   Year of Foundation and ROE of *Top Global Companies* (1997)

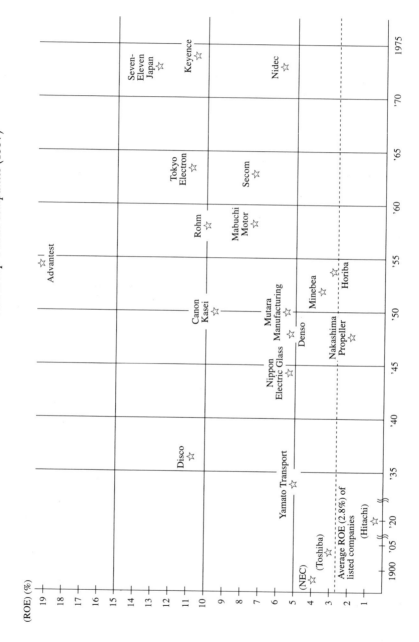

Chart 1-5   Six Strategic Partners of *Top Global Companies*

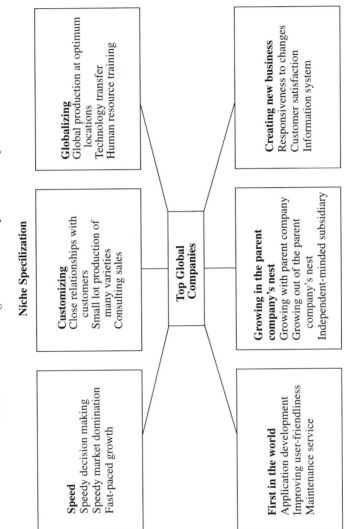

Niche Specilization

Top Global Companies

Globalizing
Global production at optimum locations
Technology transfer
Human resource training

Creating new business
Responsiveness to changes
Customer satisfaction
Information system

Customizing
Close relationships with customers
Small lot production of many varieties
Consulting sales

Growing in the parent company's nest
Growing with parent company
Growing out of the parent company's nest
Independent-minded subsidiary

Speed
Speedy decision making
Speedy market domination
Fast-paced growth

First in the world
Application development
Improving user-friendliness
Maintenance service

a) Niche specialization — speed

"Speed" is crucial to the management of companies, if they are to cope with changes in the external environment. Being "fast" and "early" permits companies to compete successfully in an era of rapid change. "Speed of decision-making" is important enough to determine the rise or fall of a company. *Top Global Companies* keep their organizations trimmed down for quick decision-making; they are not handicapped by the slow decision-making that has been frequently been mentioned as one of Japanese management's shortcomings.

Based on their market forecast several years ahead and before their competitors, **Advantest** set out to develop a high-speed tester for 64-Mb DRAM. Were it not for a speedy decision by the top management, "T5581", a global hit product, would not have been born.

The "speed of capturing the market" is vital in the industries where technological innovation forms the basis of competition. Fast introduction of products in a market before competitors move in permits a company to dominate the market at ease. For instance, **Murata Manufacturing** keeps all the production processes in-house so that the internally developed technologies do not leak out. This prevents imitation by their competitors, who must waste time catching up. During that time lag, Murata quickly captures the world market.

Accelerated growth causes medium-sized companies to face shortages of management resources including human resource. One solution to this problem is to acquire external resources. **Nidec**, for example, actively pursued headhunting and M&A (Mergers & Acquisitions) to procure the required resources and achieved rapid growth.

b) Niche specialization — customizing

Certain niches are cost inhibitive and labor intensive enough to discourage large manufacturers from participation. These niches favor companies that can make the fine adjustments necessary to meet individual customers' requirements.

Custom IC is typical of high-mix, low-volume products. Custom IC manufacturers are required to maintain close contact with customers to fully understand their requirements and develop products accordingly. **Rohm**, for example, assign their own engineers to each of their customers to thoroughly understand the customers' needs. Large manufacturers, on the contrary, would not offer such service.

The propellers of large ships are all ship-specific. **Nakashima Propeller** has a wealth of know-how that allows it to design and manufacture any large propeller. Customized products that meet individual customers' specific needs require a high level of technology and sophisticated know-how.

Keyence meets individual customers' needs differently, namely, by the effective use of general-purpose products instead of custom-made products. It provides customers with a consulting service so that the customers may become aware of the possibility of using general-purpose sensors for their specific needs. General-purpose products are more cost-effective than custom-made products.

As these examples show, companies specialized in customizing are characterized by their capabilities to offer best solutions to the specific problems of their customers.

c) Niche specialization — globalizing

Managing business on a global scale has many advantages such as the use of low labor cost, reduction of transportation cost, prompt response to overseas customers, and access to information about leading-edge technology. Many *Top Global Companies* effectively use these advantages.

Mabuchi Motor, for example, is a global enterprise, with 100% of its production offshore. Low-cost offshore production has made their costs highly competitive. Their high technological capability that has set "world standards" for 100 technical items and their insistence on "making at the lowest cost in the world" have made them a *Top Global Company*.

Minebea's global production system has eliminated the disparity between its plant in Japan and those in other Asian countries. The newest equipment developed in its mother factory in Japan has been transferred to the other Asian plants for the integrated production of sophisticated products.

Tokyo Electron has reinforced its information collection capability overseas. Their sales people and maintenance technicians working on site have been trained to study users' current activities and future directions. The first-hand information collected this way is used for their product development. Such "globalizing of the work force" is a strategy to win the competition of technological innovation.

d) First in the world

A new and unique technology is the most important asset of a company. Technological innovation, however, does not automatically make the company a *Top Global Company*. The new technology should be exploited widely so that it becomes a de facto standard.

Three exemplar companies have done this. **Yupo Corporation**, the inventor of a synthetic paper that excels in strength and water resistance, has developed a number of new markets for the new paper through intensive application development. **Disco**, the top manufacturer of ultra-thin cut-off wheels, expanded their use by developing cutting machines specifically designed for them. **Horiba** occupies 80% of the world market for the automotive emission analyzer worldwide. They have not only developed products of high quality and performance, but also offered ongoing maintenance services that have helped increase the value of their products.

Companies whose strength lies in the development of original products should be careful not to lose focus on customers. Widespread use of new products requires enhanced customer service such as customer education for the use of the products and responsive maintenance service.

e) Growing in the parent company's nest

Several subsidiary companies become *Top Global Companies* as their parent companies become global enterprises. Their strategies depend on how close they stand to their parent companies.

Canon Kasei stands close to its parent company Canon. It manufactures low cost, high quality toner cartridges for Canon's laser printers, which are sold to both the open market and to its captive customer Canon. As Canon's printers have captured global markets, Canon Kasei has also become a *Top Global Company*. The two companies share the same destiny.

Another example is **Denso**, the top manufacturer of automobile electric components in the world. It has earned its position by being a supplier to Toyota Motors, its parent company. The collapse of the interlocking relationships among automobile parts manufacturers, however, is driving Denso to apply their high caliber technological capability to new markets such as telecommunications, environmental, and LCD (Liquid Crystal Display). Thus, they are seeking to grow out of their dependence on their parent company.

Since its foundation as a subsidiary of NEC, and even before it became an independent company, **Nippon Electric Glass** had run its business with a high degree of autonomy. This has helped them to acquire the ability to develop products independently and become a prominent specialized manufacturer of cathode-ray tube glass.

f) Creating new business

The ever changing world continues to generate new needs. Breaking out of a conventional mold, some companies have created new businesses to meet these new needs, becoming leading companies in the world.

Examples of the founders of innovative businesses include **Seven-Eleven Japan**, **Yamato Transport**, and **Secom**, which created a convenience store chain, door-to-door parcel delivery service, and centralized security systems, respectively. Although they looked to pioneering companies overseas for cues to start new businesses, they established their own management systems and grew rapidly. They have all taken full advantage of their own information systems for efficient management.

Common to companies that have created new businesses is emphasis on customers. Their determination to vigorously pursue customers' convenience is exemplified by convenience stores opened 24 hours all year round, door-to-door parcel delivery service that picks up even a single package at customers' homes, or a centralized system that offers security and safety.

Chapter Two

Niche Specialization — Speed

I. Murata Manufacturing
Speedy capture of the world market with "black-boxed" technology

(*Company profile at a glance*)

Financial data (Fiscal year ended March 1998)

Sales	290,420 (million yen)
Ordinary income	30,488 (million yen)
ROE	5.7%
No. of employees	4,489

Market share in the world (estimate)

Ceramic filters	80%
Ceramic resonators	80%
Monolithic chip ceramic capacitors	50%
Microwave filters	40%
PTC thermistors	40%
EMI filters	35%

1) Leading the world market in electronic ceramic components

Murata Manufacturing is a specialized manufacturer of electronic ceramic components. Approximately, 70% of its sales revenue comes from products that have a large share in the world market. Monolithic chip ceramic capacitors have come to the top of their product lines, holding 50% of the world market. Their ceramic filters and ceramic resonators each hold 80% of the world market, while microwave filters and PTC thermistors 40%. Murata is a truly global company; it has ten plants in both domestic and offshore locations, and its overseas sales amounts to as much as 60% of the total sales.

2) Speedy capture of the market with "black-boxed" technology

The secret of Murata's success in capturing the global market with a number of their products is in their production process. Murata's products have enjoyed an established reputation for their quality. Its history is one of aiming for quality improvement. When the company was founded, they purchased raw materials from America. Those imported raw materials, however, caused variability in the products because of impurities contained in them. In order to secure raw materials of uniform quality, which were deemed indispensable to the stable production of high quality ceramic components, Murata started to produce their own raw materials. They also developed analytical instruments in cooperation with Kyoto University so as to be able to analyze the raw materials with precision. Their Materials Division is responsible for supplying raw materials of stable quality to each of their production divisions. Thus, the quality of their raw materials differentiates their products from those of their competitors.

Murata designs and builds all of its own production equipment, keeping in-house all the production processes ranging from the preparation of raw materials to the firing of finished ceramic products. This enables them to safeguard proprietary production know-how in a black box, which makes it harder for their competitors to imitate. This also permits production cost information to stay in the black box and makes it difficult for Murata's customers to negotiate price concessions.

Thus, by "black-boxed" proprietary technology, Murata has been able to capture the world market in a short time before its competitors catch up. The speed at which Murata has captured the market is the key to its success in climbing to the top of its niche in the world market.

3) Developing new products by combining existing technologies

Murata has accumulated a good stock of technology through their expertise in their own raw materials. Combining different areas of such technology, they have developed "module products" that possess compound functions. Module products give customers the benefit of multiple functions. The sale of value-added module products, in which Murata's ceramic components are combined with IC chips and other components bought from outside vendors, has grown rapidly. Microwave filters for cell phones and ceramic resonators are examples of such products developed by combining technologies.

Since the prices of individual ceramic components are low, they have to be sold in a large quantity for them to become a viable business. Technology combination is an effective way to expand the application and therefore the market of ceramic components.

4) Accelerating R&D by scientific management

Technology innovation takes place at a breathtaking pace in electronics. This makes the speed of R&D crucial to success in this industry. Murata applies "scientific management" to its R&D to increase the speed. As technology advances, new products are introduced and the prices of old products fall. Manufacturers of components, therefore, have to keep developing new components that satisfy the new needs of their customers who make finished products.

In order to increase the success rate of their product development, Murata screens R&D projects according to their long-term plan. They then identify technical elements necessary for specific product development and decide which of those technical elements are to be developed in-house. The selected technical themes are assigned to 25 development groups, each of which is held accountable for completing the development of a specific technical theme by a predetermined deadline. Murata's R&D management is thus characterized by the tight management of individual development groups in order to accelerate product development.

This R&D management method, however, interferes with information exchange among development groups, and may ultimately reduce the efficiency of the whole technology development organization. A remedy for this problem is a mechanism that has been established to facilitate information sharing among the development groups. The monthly technical meetings of each group are attended by members of other groups. Furthermore, technical reports and case studies for both successes and failures have been compiled in a database form. Such sharing of knowledge and know-how can eliminate potential redundancy in basic research and increase the efficiency of the whole technology development organization. As a way to motivate their engineers, Murata encourages them to make presentations at professional associations' meetings and pursue doctorates.

Managing each of the development groups individually is an ingenious way to control R&D, which otherwise tends to nurture a lack of discipline. This is the reason why Murata has succeeded in developing a number of products that have captured a large share of the global market.

5) Matrix management for strict cost control

Technology-oriented companies tend to be lax with financial management. Despite its strong technology orientation, however, Murata has implemented strict cost management at each production step. Its employees are required to be conscious of the profit and loss of their own divisions.

Murata Manufacturing and its group companies have established a matrix of more than 2,500 "management units" by product and by process, with each unit responsible for its own profit and loss. Murata has referred to this financial management system as "matrix management". It is intended to eliminate waste through strict profit and loss control at each production step so that production costs may be reduced to a practical limit. Their superb cost competitiveness is a result of this matrix management system. Matrix management is used by many manufacturing companies now, but Murata has used it in its original form since the 1960s.

Traditionally, all the capital investment proposals by "management units" were submitted to the president of the company for his approval. As the business expanded, however, this approval procedure led to slow decision-making. In order to solve this problem, part of the president's authority was delegated to the division managers, who were then authorized to approve capital investments of 2 billion yen or less.

6) Speedy response to technology advancement through wholly owned subsidiaries

Almost all of the companies that comprise Murata Manufacturing Group are wholly owned subsidiaries. This is not accidental but intentional. Each of the subsidiaries does not belong to a specific division of the head office, but takes care of the business of multiple divisions. Like the head office, each subsidiary has specific "management units" assigned to it by product and by process. As a result, the head office and the subsidiaries are integrated into a single seamless organization.

In the electronics industry, incessant technical innovation results in frequent changes in production processes. In Murata Manufacturing Group, a new production process can be readily adopted only by making changes in "management units" that encompass both the head office and subsidiaries on a common basis.

The human resource of the group is also managed in a unified way throughout. The unified wage and qualification systems ensure smooth transfer of personnel within the group.

Murata has converted their business units into subsidiaries so as to make each operation clearly accountable for its own profit and loss. The important thing is that those subsidiaries are wholly owned and

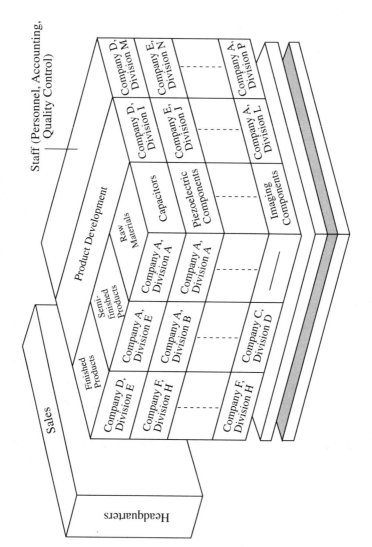

Chart 2-1   Matrix Management Concept

Notes: Company A, Division A, etc, indicate each process or department of both headquarters and subsidiaries
(Source: Nihon Keizai Shimbun, 20 February 1988)

integral members of Murata Manufacturing Group. This is to eliminate potential disparity and estrangement between the head office and the subsidiaries and ensure prompt response of the whole group to technical innovations.

7) Effective use of limited human resource

Medium-sized companies have to find ways to effectively use their limited human resource. Murata strives to increase the abilities of the whole company by increasing the special capabilities of individual employees. When they reach twenty-eight years of age, Murata's employees are asked to choose their "principal job" out of more than 20 jobs and begin training to become a specialist in their principal job. This training lasts throughout their employment, although they may receive temporary assignments outside of their principal job. Thus, Murata's employees are encouraged to become members of the specialist group within the company through the "principal job" system instead of becoming a generalist of limited capabilities. Raising the quality of the human resources to overcome the handicap of the limited quantity is a noteworthy way for a medium-sized company to compete with large corporations.

8) Pioneering overseas fund raising

In the 1970s in Japan, it was not easy for a medium-sized company to raise funds. In 1976, Murata Manufacturing became the first Japanese company listed on the Singapore Stock Exchange. The locally raised funds permitted their subsidiary in Singapore to enjoy steady expansion of its business. Murata deserves the honor of being the second medium-sized company after Sony to have raised capital overseas.

Thus, Murata has managed their finances as well as production and sales on a global scale since the early days. The management know-how they have accumulated over many years supports their business overseas and distinguishes them from their competitors.

II. Nidec
Rapid growth by M&A

(Company profile at a glance)

Financial data (Fiscal year ended March 1998)

Sales	97,957 (million yen)
Ordinary income	8,802 (million yen)
ROE	6.1%
No. of employees	1,097

Market share in the world (estimate)

HDD spindle motors	70%

1) No. 1 supplier of spindle motors for HDD

Nidec is a manufacturer of small precision DC motors. Its spindle motors for HDD (Hard Disk Drive) hold a 70% share of the world market. Their motors are also used for magnetic optical disk drives, CD-ROM drives, and laser printers. They also manufacture small AC motors for copying machines, small axial fans for cooling electronic parts, and a variety of electric power units. Thus, their business is about what rotates and what moves.

2) Specializing in business fields shunned by other companies; capturing the domestic market by reverse landing

Nidec was founded in 1973 to launch the business of small DC motors which had been shunned by many other companies because of their depressed prices. As an obscure manufacturer in the field, Nidec encountered serious difficulties in finding domestic customers for their products. Nidec then turned to the US market where users were expected to purchase products from a supplier on their own merits (e.g. product quality and delivery), disregarding the name or history of the supplier. Nidec's energetic sales promotion resulted in acquiring orders from IBM and other leading companies. Their reputation in the US market in turn prompted an increase in the number of domestic customers to purchase Nidec's products. As Nidec's example shows, "reverse landing" on domestic soil is an effective gate opener to domestic customers who in general are reluctant to accept newcomers as their suppliers.

Since then, Nidec has grown into a global enterprise, building plants in the US, Singapore, Thailand, Taiwan, China, and the Philippines. New companies can learn from Nidec's strategy, which was to select a business filled with little competition and solidify its foundation in a receptive market.

Chart 2-2   History of Nidec's Sales

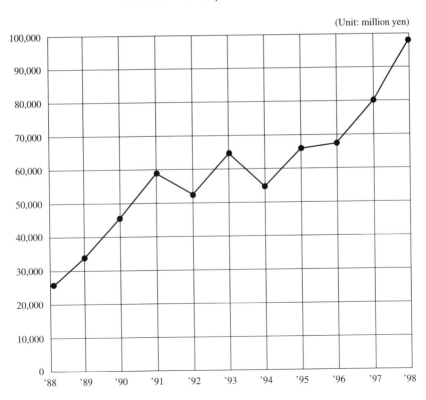

(Unit: million yen)

3) M&A for saving time for growth

Nidec has grown remarkably fast. Nidec's sales quadrupled in the 10 years since 1988 and its annual sales almost reached a landmark of 100 billion yen in 1998. It was a phenomenal achievement made in less than 30 years from its foundation.

Nidec's rapid growth owes greatly to M&A (Mergers and Acquisitions). Relying only on their own resources would have limited their expansion. Aggressive M&A to acquire outer resources enabled Nidec to achieve their phenomenal growth. In 1988, Nidec was listed in the First Sections of the Osaka Stock Exchange and of the Kyoto Stock Exchange. The funds raised in the stock market were then used for M&A, which was done in a rapid succession as shown below. This was a strategy to save the time that would have been required for growth.

February 1984	Purchased the Axial Flow Fan Division of Torin Corp. in the U.S.A.
January 1989	Equity participation in DC Park Co., Ltd. to launch power supply business
March 1989	Purchased Shinano Tokki Co., Ltd.
May 1991	Nidec America Corp. purchased Power General
January 1992	Purchased the High Precision Composite Parts Division of Seagate Japan
October 1993	Purchased Masaka Electronic Co., Ltd. and merged it with Ibaragi Nidec Corp.
February 1995	Underwrote an increase in the capital and became the owner of Shimpo Industries Co., Ltd.
March 1996	Daisan Kogyo was merged with Shimpo Industries
March 1997	Read Electronics became a subsidiary
March 1997	Tosok Corp. became a Nidec affiliate through purchase of shares
February 1998	Became the top shareholder of Copal by acquiring 18% of the outstanding stock
May 1998	Established a joint venture with Shibaura Mechatronics Corp. to succeed the electric motors business from the latter

(Source: *Pocket History of Nidec*, pp. 48–49; Nihon Keizai Shimbun)

Nidec has succeeded in the niche markets they initially targeted. For further growth, however, they needed to be capable of competing in larger markets that would allow them to expand the applications of small motors. Acquiring Tosok, Shibaura Mechatronics, and Copal was a stepping stone to making inroads into the automobile and house appliance markets for motors.

Product development can be accelerated by acquiring a company that already has the technology needed. Furthermore, the production facilities of the buyer and the acquired company can be combined to accelerate production start-up. M&A has played an important role in the strategy of Nidec who has used "speed" as leverage to carve out niche markets.

4) Speedy and flexible product development

Until the late 1970s, the spindle and motor of a HDD were separate parts, the former driven by the latter by a belt. This design suffered from the space required and heat generated. In 1978, Nidec started a project to develop a small spindle motor in which the spindle and the motor were united into a single unit. In cooperation with manufacturers of HDDs, they explored the use of brushless DC motors, to which their competitors at that time were not paying attention. In order to win severe competition, Nidec strived to accommodate all the details of HDD manufacturers' requests by repeatedly modifying stereotypes, which were submitted to prospective customers for their criticism. This flexible response to customers' demands kept Nidec ahead of large companies competing with them. It helped them win HDD manufacturers' collaboration in the project completed in 1979 the first successful model of a high precision spindle motor for HDD.

Nidec knew well that fast-paced technical innovation for HDD quickly makes a model perfected through long hours of development obsolete. In their prototyping, therefore, speed of delivery was given preference over quality and cost. This strategy was supported by their customers and enabled Nidec to keep adding new names to their customer list. Nidec's example demonstrates that speed and flexibility are indispensable to creating a competitive advantage in markets where fast-paced technological innovation takes place.

5) Three mottos to drive rapid growth

The rapid growth of Nidec cannot be attributed solely to M&A. The energy created by the people and organization of Nidec also played a role.

Shigenobu Nagamori, president and founder of Nidec, is adamant that his employees strive to be the best in whatever they are engaged in. He appeals to his employees to double their efforts compared to Nidec's competitors; if the competitors try twice as hard, Nidec will try four times harder. This was a way to supplement Nidec's limited resources. All the employees of Nidec are indoctrinated with the three company mottos: "Passion, zeal, persistence", "Work hard, using the mind", and "Act immediately, do without fail, complete the work".

Nidec Group holds board meetings and managing directors' meetings only on Saturdays and Sundays, work in the offices and plants taking precedence over the meetings. President Nagamori is an extremely hardworking leader of the company, working every weekday and weekend throughout the year except for a visit to a shrine on the morning of New Year's Day.

Nidec pays no attention to school grades when hiring new graduates. They rate people who act on their own initiative higher than those who are good at processing given tasks and producing good enough results like students who score well in school. Newly hired workers are indoctrinated with the company mottos and taught to strive to be the best. Thus, Nidec's energy comes from the spirit of the three mottos that is shared by all the members of the Nidec Group.

6) Human resource management for growth

One of the issues resulting from Nidec's rapid growth is how to fulfill human resource requirements. Being a young company, Nidec always has positions to fill, especially those of managers. In order to solve this problem, Nidec has recruited people from a variety of industrial fields. Those recruits now occupy 40% of the total employees of Nidec. Thus, Nidec actively pursues external resources including human resources.

Chart 2-3   Business Contents of Overseas Factories

Nidec's Subsidiaries Overseas	Business Contents
Nidec America	Sales and production of small precision fan and electric power units; Sales of small precision motors
Nidec Singapore	Sales of small precision motors, small precision fan, electronic products and parts; Production and sales of pivot assemblies
Nidec Electronics (Thailand)	Production and sales of small precision motors
Nidec Taiwan	Production and sales of small precision fan; Global procurement of materials and parts
Nidec (H.K.)	Global procurement of materials and parts; Sales of small precision fan and small precision motors
Nidec (Dalian)	Production and sales of small precision motors, small precision fan and electric power units, and of their parts
Nidec Electronics (Europe)	Sales of small precision motors, small precision fan, and electric power units
Nidec Philippines	Production of small precision motors

(Source: *Pocket History of Nidec*, p. 50)

Nidec pays close attention on how to motivate its employees. The company rewards employees strictly on their own merits; employees are appraised according to their capabilities, achievements, and performance rather than their years of service and age. The company sometimes allows people to skip a few steps in their climb up the corporate ladder. Some positions are offered openly within the company to invite ambitious employees to apply for them.

Employees may make significant contributions to the company's profit by improving the way business is done or developing new customers and markets. In 1996, "Contribution-to-Profit Grand Prix" was established to recognize such contributions. The winner of the highest honor of the "Diamond Special Prize" receives 10 million yen in cash. Similarly, Nidec in the same year established a stock option plan to share part of their profit with employees. Such human resource management has supported Nidec's growth.

7) "Made in the market" — offshore strategy

Since the Plaza Accord, many customers of Nidec have moved their plants offshore. In order to satisfy their needs, Nidec has also built offshore plants one after another. Those production plants located near their customers have allowed Nidec to respond quickly to customers' claims or changes in the market's needs. Nidec refers to this basic strategy as "made in the market" strategy.

Nidec's offshore production has now reached 70% of their total production. According to their financial report at the end of the third quarter of 1998, all of their offshore plants except the one in the Philippines made a profit. This shows that Nidec's offshore strategy is working. As the offshore production ratio has increased, Nidec's domestic operations have shifted their focus to R&D and the production of value-added products.

III. Advantest
Capturing memory tester market with speedy management

(*Company profile at a glance*)

Financial data (Fiscal year ended March 1998)

Sales	233,620 (million yen)
Ordinary income	67,400 (million yen)
ROE	19.9%
No. of employees	1,552

Market share in the world (estimate)

Memory testers	60%

1) Largest manufacturer of semiconductor testers

Advantest is the largest manufacturer of semiconductor testers. Their main products include semiconductor testers represented by memory testers and electronic measuring instruments such as digital voltage monitors. They also manufacture electron beam lithography systems. With the success of their 250 MHz high speed memory tester named T5581 for 64 MB DRAM, Advantest holds 60% of the memory tester market in the world.

2) Capturing the market with the speed of product introduction

In the early 1990s, Advantest's share in the US market dropped as a result of their slow development of the technologies used in logic testers. In 1992, however, they decided to start a project to develop a 250 MHz high-speed memory tester referred to as T5581 for 64 MB DRAM. This decision was based on their forecast which predicted that T5581 was to be put into full production in several years. At that time, memory testers being developed by their competitors were only as fast as 60 MHz, which made T5581 the fastest tester under development. In addition, T5581 was going to be a compact high

Chart 2-4   Financial Performance and R&D Expense of Advantest

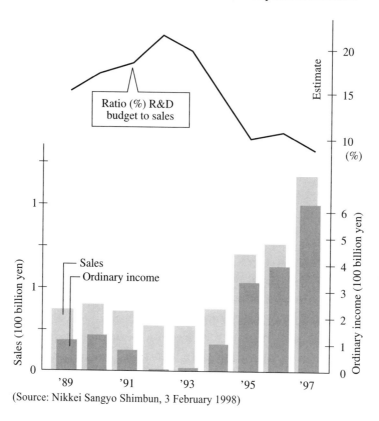

Ratio (%) R&D
budget to sales

Estimate

Sales (100 billion yen)

Ordinary income (100 billion yen)

Sales
Ordinary income

'89   '91   '93   '95   '97

(Source: Nikkei Sangyo Shimbun, 3 February 1998)

quality tester of low power consumption meeting the requirements of semiconductor manufacturers.

At the end of 1993, the first prototype was made and delivered to semiconductor manufacturers. This was made possible by standardizing all the assembly boards to shorten the assembly time. Put into full production in 1995, T5581 dominated the market of high speed memory testers in a very short time.

Thanks to the success of T5581, Advantest's financial report for the third quarter of 1998 showed that sales and ordinary income increased by as much as 50% and 70%, respectively, compared to those of the same quarter of the previous year.

The speed of the development and introduction of T5581 was what permitted Advantest to dominate the global market.

3) Speedy decision-making

Decisions concerning company management, as well as products, are quickly made within the Advantest organization. Until the beginning of the 1990s, however, Advantest's management was far from being speedy. With Fujitsu as the major shareholder in Advantest and with engineers in control of the company, Advantest had been characterized by its laid-back atmosphere. In 1989, when Fujitsu dispatched Hiroshi Oura to preside over Advantest, the company was a happy participant in the bubble economy, excessively investing in real estate. As a result, when the semiconductor memory market fell in the early 1990s, Advantest's performance deteriorated, coming close to reporting a loss.

In order to get over this crisis, President Oura set out to restructure the company along his vision that Advantest's mission is to "support at the leading edge the leading edge technologies embodied in semiconductors". His austere measures included layoffs that lasted as long as nine months, leasing of 300 employees, merger and closure of offices, and elimination of unprofitable products. Despite all of this, however, the R&D budget was kept intact for the future.

President Oura spent time in talking to employees, emphasizing the importance of speedy management. The time from the kickoff of a product development project to the delivery of a prototype was greatly shortened by delegating authorization power down the chain of command. His efforts resulted in a turnaround in the culture of the company, and the once laid-back Advantest turned itself into a speed-oriented organization.

In 1992, when the restructuring had reached its goal, he decided to kick off the T5581 project to develop a high speed memory tester ahead of competitors. It was a brave decision in view of Advantest's poor performance at that time, its ordinary income as low as one tenth of that of the previous year. Were it not for his decision to keep investing in R&D in growth areas, T5581 and its success would never have become a reality. They are the fruit of his speedy management.

4) Go first, pull ahead

Advantest's speedy product developments start with information gathering. When visiting semiconductor customers, Advantest's sales people are always accompanied by engineers responsible for product development, so that customers' needs may be fully understood. Direct contact with customers gives them opportunities to learn customers' know-how such as the specific testing systems they use. Upon customers' request, information is sent back in real time by a personal computer to Advantest's R&D Division. Thus, bringing their R&D close to customers, Advantest pulls itself ahead of competition.

It is predicted that a 256 MB DRAM will be put into full production around the year 2000. In view of this, Advantest has been developing a memory tester to be ready for this next generation memory chip. Ahead of their competitors, Advantest has already developed a 1 GHz ultra high speed tester named T5591 for Rambus DRAM and cache memory. The prototype of T5591 was delivered to several DRAM manufacturers.

With system LSI just around the corner, Advantest is developing an electron beam lithograph system that would permit semiconductor manufacturers to burn LSI circuitries on silicon wafers with the electron beam. This system is expected to become a new tool for ultra fine fabrication that would take us beyond the limit of conventional lithograph systems.

As for electronic measuring instruments, Advantest succeeded in developing a portable microwave spectrum analyzer called U3661 for the first time in the world. They have also been engaged in the development of W-CDMA spectrum analysis technique that adopts IMT-2000, the next generation standard for mobile transmission.

These developments for establishing next generation technologies also demonstrate Advantest's strategy of "Go first, pull ahead".

5) Sole winner with a strategic niche focus

In hi-tech industries, strong companies are getting stronger, reaping a richer harvest. Among them are many specialized companies with their focus on a specific niche. Examples are Microsoft and Intel, which have become dominant suppliers in the world in their OS (Operating System) and MPU (Micro Processing Unit), respectively. Another example is Advantest which has become a sole winner in the high speed tester market, holding a 60% share of the world market.

In contrast, the performance of the overly diversified domestic electronic conglomerates has rapidly deteriorated. Especially worsening is their semiconductor business. This is a clear sign of big companies' shortcomings that include slow decision-making, lack of technology innovation, and lack of flexibility in their response to customers' requirements.

Advantest has become a sole winner in its niche as a result of their far-sighted investment in carefully selected technologies. This strategy has allowed them to shorten the time for the development of the products customers would need. It is a model strategy that leads to a sure win in the hi-tech industry.

Chapter Three

Niche Specialization — Customizing

I. Rohm
Willing to do what big companies are reluctant to do

(*Company profile at a glance*)

Financial data (Fiscal year ended March 1998)

Sales	272,839 (million yen)
Ordinary income	61,352 (million yen)
ROE	10.3%
No. of employees	2,542

Market share worldwide (estimate)

Print heads for facsimile machines	34%

1) Custom ICs

Rohm is a semiconductor manufacturer of high earning power. Their print heads for facsimile machines have the top share of the market worldwide, with their small-signal transistors, silicon diodes, laser diodes, and resistors also having a large market share. They also make LED, LCD, and sensors. Their expertise in designing and crafting custom ICs has been well appreciated by the market.

Chart 3-1   Rohm's Domestic Market Share (1997)

Small-signal transistors	42.2%
Print heads for facsimile machines	41.0%
Silicon diodes	36.3%
Laser diodes	28.0%
Chip resistors	26.2%
Power transistors	18.8%
Liner ICs (for industrial and civil use)	16.5%
LED	6.6%

(Source: Nikkei Database)

2) "Willing to do what big companies are reluctant to do"

Big companies are reluctant to accept time-consuming jobs or keep old technologies. Rohm saw opportunities there and has made successful business out of those niches. They have been most successful in customizing ICs to customers' specifications.

Rohm assigns a dedicated engineer to each of the customers' products on the table. This is to maintain close relationship with customers from the designing stage of their products and to understand specific IC requirements for the products. It is Rohm's policy to integrate the fine details of customers' requirements into the process of designing and crafting optimum custom ICs. Their advanced designing capability and production technology permit them to respond to the diverse requirements of customers.

Rohm has drawn customers in by showing its flexibility in accommodating customers' specifications and perfecting customized ICs down to the fine details of their requests. Rohm's excellent example demonstrates how a small or medium-sized company can be successful by being "willing to do what big companies are reluctant to do".

3) Profiting from old technologies

Large manufacturers are obsessed by leading edge technology. Many of them discontinue products that are based on technologies a couple of generations old. They do so for the reason that those products have lost shine in the marketplace, even if the market still needs them.

Rohm has done the opposite in the production of **memories**; they have deliberately stayed away from leading-edge **memories**. In the **memories** discontinued by large manufacturers Rohm sees the opportunity to sign contracts with them and become an OEM supplier to them. This arrangement permits Rohm to obtain the know-how that large manufacturers have developed over many years, and do it for free. Furthermore, Rohm fabricates its own production equipment to reduce the production cost.

This is the reason why Rohm can make several-generations-old products at low costs. Rohm is an expert gleaning pieces of technology abandoned by large manufacturers and making business out of them.

After the first step of technology acquisition, Rohm transfers the equipment and production know-how from the mother plant to domestic subsidiaries and finally to overseas subsidiaries. This is to reduce the production costs as much as possible. As a result, Rohm can still keep providing the market with cost-competitive products.

Since electronic products have short lives in the market, the company ahead of the pack does not necessarily enjoy a lucrative reward for the product it has introduced into the market. In light of this risk, Rohm does not jump at leading-edge technologies, but makes highly profitable business out of products and technologies large manufacturers have abandoned. It is a marvelous strategy.

4) Profitability in preference to sales revenue

Small companies cannot compete against large companies on the basis of the amount of profit. Rohm gained a high earning capacity by making profitability its top priority over sales revenue.

Rohm's financial report for the fiscal year ending in March 1990 showed that the sales revenue had increased by 10.6% but that the operating profit decreased by as much as 36.1%. This gave the opportunity for Rohm to switch its priority from the expansion of sales volume regardless of cost to the improvement of profitability. Unprofitable products were listed up, and one-third of the whole product line was discontinued. Furthermore, the prices of some products were reduced. Half of the executives were fired, bearing the blame for the discount in sales at the expense of profit.

The drastic restructuring paid off, and Rohm transformed itself into a highly profitable company characterized by a high ratio of operating profit to sales revenue. Such drastic restructuring would have been impossible in a big company.

5) High quality to win the market's confidence

Low cost is not the only thing Rohm offers to the market. Their striving for the highest quality resulted in the QLP (Quality Leader Program) Prize from AT&T, Q1 (Quality No. 1) Prize from Ford, and Engineering Achievement Prize from IEEE.

Under the motto of "Quality First", Rohm has paid close attention to four basic elements (4M) of quality control, that is, Man, Machine, Materials, and Method, and strived to keep 4M in top-notch condition. This is the reason why Rohm's products are known for their high quality as well as low cost in the market.

Rohm is not just satisfied by its success with the products and technologies abandoned by large manufacturers. They are also actively pursuing the development of new products such as next generation memories for multimedia. They know they cannot be complacent and have to look ahead, if they are to continue to be a winner in the rapidly changing electronics industry.

6) Motivation management

The morale of Rohm's employees is very high. This is attributed to Rohm's unique human resource management designed for maintaining an energetic organization.

At Rohm, the company's monthly performance by divisions and by products is disclosed to the employees. The performance is evaluated with various financial indices such as sales revenue, cost ratio, claim ratio, and profit. Each division's ranking is shown at the end of the monthly financial report, so that each division's earnings and ranking are obvious to everyone. This open disclosure system within the company is to stimulate competition among the divisions.

As Kenichiro Sato, president of Rohm, has stated in public, lifetime employment is not a rule at Rohm. The employees are rewarded or punished according to their performance. Ability and competence have been the sole basis in Rohm's wage system. For example, as early as in 1966, Rohm's staff began to receive salary on an annual basis. Employees who had accomplished outstanding achievements are recognized with honor and cash rewards, the highest prize being the ten million yen Diamond Prize. These systems help motivate employees and maintain the vitality of the company.

While the performance of the company is vigorously controlled by numbers, Rohm makes sure to keep an open atmosphere throughout the organization. The office of the president is open to everyone, so that anyone can visit him and express his or her opinion. The president sometimes simply asks employees to join him in a get-together after work. He also encourages person-to-person direct communication among employees. He is skeptical about the efficacy of the now popular electronic mail. Thus, Rohm's management skillfully motivates employees by applying a modern administrative method, on the one hand, and by appealing to their emotion, on the other hand.

II. Nakashima Propeller
Unique know-how for small lot production of many varieties

(Company profile at a glance)

Financial data (Fiscal year ended November 1997)

Sales	10,184 (million yen)
Ordinary income	53 (million yen)
ROE	1.72%
No. of employees	342

Market share worldwide (estimate)

Marine propellers	40%

1) Global no. 1 manufacturer of marine propellers located in a local city

Nakashima Propeller is located in the city of Okayama. They specialize in the manufacture of marine propellers for ships and boats of all sorts and all sizes. Some ships are as large as several hundred thousand tons. They have a 40% market share in marine propellers in the world. They were the first to introduce the Keyless Propeller and the High Skew Propeller into the market. The latter enabled significant noise reduction. They have also applied the technology that was developed for manufacturing propellers to other products. Examples include a hanging bell called Melody Bell, which produces musical sound, and artificial joints made of titanium.

2) Foresight and unique know-how

In 1962, Nakashima shifted its focus from small boats to large ships. This decision was based on their prediction of a shipbuilding boom for large vessels. Once the decision was made, they sent engineers to the Ship Research Center to master the technology necessary for manufacturing propellers for large vessels. They also invested heavily into building proper facilities. Thus, they systematically prepared themselves for the coming boom.

Nakashima was ready when it actually happened as they had predicted. Their careful preparation permitted them to respond and launch themselves into the global market of marine propellers.

Propellers for large vessels are more than 10 m in diameter and weigh more than 30 tons. Molds to cast such propellers are huge. Besides, since the propeller for one particular vessel is shaped differently from that of another, each propeller requires a specific mold. Selection and mixing of materials for giant molds needs unique know-how. Nakashima has accumulated such know-how through the manufacture of all sorts of propellers for large vessels. It is this know-how that has permitted Nakashima to adapt itself to small lot production of many varieties and that has prevented competitors from catching up.

The production of propellers includes a process to cast molten metals into molds. Because of the poor working environment and low productivity of this process, large shipbuilding companies closed their foundries one after another and sent orders to Nakashima. This caused a surge of orders. Nakashima is now developing a system that would allow them to automate the casting process. It is their foresight and unique know-how that has made Nakashima a *Top Global Company*.

3) CAD/CAM for labor cost reduction, craftsmanship for the finishing touch

The shape of the propeller for a vessel is determined by the specifications of that particular vessel. The shape of one propeller, therefore, is different from another. As a result, designing a propeller in the past required an enormous amount of numerical data and calculation. In order to solve this problem, Nakashima decided to develop a CAD system for the optimum designing of propellers and completed it in 1973. While typical designing work had taken some 10 days, the new system took only 15 minutes to finish the same job.

After the basic shape of a propeller is formed by casting, three-dimensional machining is used to carve the cast into the final shape. In cooperation with Toshiba Machine, Nakashima developed a three-axis control machining center that could automatically fashion the fins of the propeller as drawn on a blueprint. Later, this machine became the model for the present five-axis control machining center.

It is not without reason that Nakashima could develop such excellent designing systems and machinery. When the Second World War ended, Nakashima was entrusted to preserve and edit drawings and technical data which had been owned by the former Navy and the Ship Research Center of the Ministry of Transport. This precious technical data formed the basis for Nakashima in developing their new manufacturing technologies.

The CAD/CAM systems permitted Nakashima to automate the manufacturing processes from designing to machining, except for casting. This automation, however, does not eliminate the final step of fine-tuning by a skilled craftsman. He actually boards the vessel equipped with a new propeller and makes fine adjustments in order to minimize the noise generated by the propeller. Thus, Nakashima combines the modern CAD/CAM technology with craftsmanship to produce propellers of the highest quality for global customers.

4)   New propellers

Nakashima has been active in developing new types of propellers. Until the 1960s, the propeller and the shaft had been joined together by wedging a key between the two. In this design, there was a danger that the key might suffer from fatigue and a resultant excessive force might break the shaft. In order to solve this problem, Nakashima pursued the idea of eliminating the key and succeeded in developing the Keyless Propeller in 1971. The Keyless Propeller is now used on ships all around the world.

In 1981, Nakashima developed the High Skew Propeller, with which the noise and vibration attributed to propellers was reduced by as much as 40%. Noise reduction is essential to military ships, including submarines. Noise reduction also leads to fuel saving, which is crucial to large vessels consuming a large amount of fuel. It is therefore natural that Nakashima's High Skew Propeller has been adopted by large vessels all around the world.

Nakashima has also actively pursued overseas technologies to improve their own, since technology is the very basis for solidifying the company's position in the market. The market of propellers is small and therefore does not attract large companies. The success of Nakashima demonstrates that small or medium-sized companies can enjoy a competitive advantage over large companies if they carve out a niche like Nakashima's.

5)   Diverse applications

The sound muffling technology developed for propellers has found a very different application. It was used to commercialize Melody Bell, a hanging bell that produces a musical sound. This is really a result of reverse thinking. Nakashima also commercialized artificial joints made of titanium by applying the knowledge of materials and three-dimensional machining technology developed for propellers.

In 1987, Nakashima founded Systems Nakashima Co., Ltd. to market the CAD/CAM systems they had developed through the designing and manufacturing of propellers. Nakashima is expanding their business through active applications of the technology they have accumulated.

III. Keyence
"Consulting Sales" and "Fabless Production" for high profits

(Company profile at a glance)

Financial data (Fiscal year ended March 1998)

Sales	65,036 (million yen)
Ordinary income	28,644 (million yen)
ROE	11.0%
No. of employees	1,117

Chart 3-2 Historical Performance of Keyence:
Sales, Operating Income, and Ratio of Operating Income to Sales

(Unit: million yen)

Fiscal year ending	Sales	Operating Income	Operating Income/Sales (%)
March 1995	37,302	14,209	38.1%
March 1996	46,608	19,405	41.6%
March 1997	55,167	24,452	44.3%
March 1998	65,036	28,484	43.8%

1) Leading company of FA sensors

The main products of Keyence are sensors for FA (Factory Automation) including optic, laser, ultrasonic, and magnetic sensors. They also produce measuring and controlling instruments such as controllers, micrometers, bar code readers, microscopes, machine vision systems, and marking instruments. Due to the versatility of their products, as many as 50,000 companies have become their customers.

2) Niche specialization for high profits

Keyence's vision is summarized in their motto "Maximum profits with minimum capital". As a matter of fact, their earning power is awesome; the ratio of operating income to sales revenue for fiscal 1996, 1997, and 1998 exceeded 40%. Labor-saving FA sensors are fashionable products, to be sure, but very few companies constantly achieve a ratio of operating income to sales revenue more than ten times the average of the listed companies. Keyence's high earning power truly meets the world standard.

Keyence is guided by its excellent product and market strategies in the niches it has carved out. They do not participate in large markets where they have to compete with large companies. Typical markets they select and develop products for are around one and a half billion yen. In these small markets, Keyence's sales force works diligently according to a carefully thought out plan until they dominate the market. Since there are few competitors in those markets, price erosion can be avoided, which allows Keyence to maintain a high profitability for a long period. This is the secret of Keyence's high profitability.

If a market expands and becomes too competitive, Keyence withdraws from the market by its own decision, for the profitability of products in such a market is reduced. Keyence's strategy is to dominate the markets where they see considerable demands but little competition. It is a model strategy for small and medium-sized companies.

3) Effective use of versatile products to meet individual needs

Keyence sells its products directly to the customers through its own sales force without using sales agents. Keyence's salesmen are trained to give customers advice on how to select and use their products. This "consulting sales" is the way Keyence expands its customer base.

Keyence sells versatile products; they do not make custom products. Their salesmen are expected to help customers find ways to adopt versatile products. In a typical customer visit, a salesman suggests how the customer may use versatile FA sensors to make production lines more efficient. The customer learns from the salesman new ways to improve efficiency by using versatile sensors, which are more cost-effective than custom-made sensors. Through such consulting sales activities, Keyence's salesmen find and expand applications of versatile products. Besides they are cheaper than custom-made products, versatile products can be shipped as soon as orders are received.

Many companies customize their products to meet individual customers' needs. In the light of this, Keyence's market approach is

Chart 3-3   Production System of Keyence

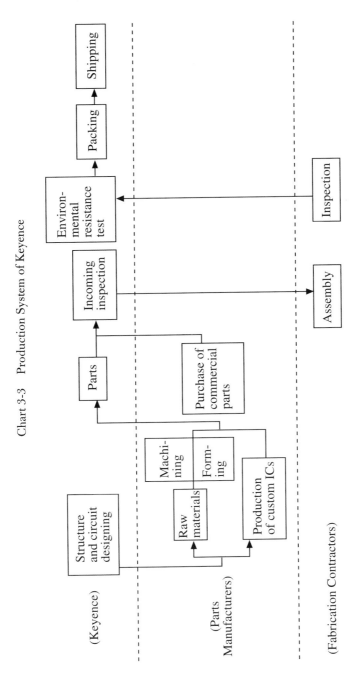

(Source: Keyence Comprehensive Financial Statements, March 1998, p. 9)

unique in that they explore applications of versatile products to specific needs.

4) Efficient management of fabless company

Keyence is a fabless company; they do not own fabrication facilities. They do their own planning and designing of products, but actual production is contracted out to supporting manufacturers. Since they can dispense with large capital investment and maintenance expense, they can minimize the fixed cost. Furthermore, the lack of fixed production facilities makes it easier for them to respond to changes in the market and develop products in a timely fashion. In order to store production technology, however, they have new products and highly proprietary products made first at their subsidiary Kurepo Co., Ltd. and later contracted out to supporting manufacturers.

Chart 3-4   Keyence's Recent Product Development

1994	March	Smallest laser market in the world
	July	Laser focus displacement meter
1995	May	PC card data collection system
	July	Microscope for shape measurement
	November	Smallest image recognition instrument in the world
1996	June	Digital optic fiber sensor
	September	Smallest ratio control amplifier in the world
	December	New CCD laser displacement sensor
1997	April	Smallest radio controller in the world
	September	Smallest laser bar code reader in the world

(Source: *The Way a Company Evolves — Keyence*, Diamond, p. 89)

Keyence's products are easy to use. They are neither multifunctional nor of high performance. This is to minimize both development and production cost.

Fabless production requires close communication between the head office and the contractors. The Production Management Department of Keyence is there to facilitate communication and ensure close working relationships between the head office and the contractors.

Fabless production allows a company to concentrate its management resources on its core business. It has allowed Keyence to concentrate on and enhance their core competence of product planning and development.

5) "Customer information sheet" for product development

Keyence excels at developing products that appeal to latent needs. Their salesmen are expected fully to investigate the latent needs of customers. They ascertain such needs and new opportunities for applying their products during their sales calls and record them in the "customer information sheet". The huge amount of information deposited by the salesmen everyday is used to develop products that would satisfy the latent needs of customers. This is the reason why their products sell well when introduced into the market. Information helpful for negotiating with customers is communicated to all the salesmen to raise their sales activities to a higher level. Thus, the customer information sheet is used both for product development and for sales promotion. This integration of sales and product development has become one of the company's strengths.

6) Performance-based reward system to boost salesmen's morale

Since Keyence's direct sales system hinges on the morale of its salesmen, many tools are used to boost their morale. Each of the company's sales offices receives a report every month that shows the monthly gross profit target and actual performance of each sales office and each sales group and their ranking. The report is posted on the wall so that every salesman can see how the office and the group he belongs to is doing.

Each of the salesmen receives individual performance reports. These reports are to boost his morale, because he knows his salary and bonus depend on his performance.

The average length of service of the company's male employees is less than six years. This means non-performing salesmen cannot survive in Keyence. The shrewd performance-based reward system is the backbone of the powerful sales force of the company.

Chapter Four

Niche Specialization — Globalizing

I. Mabuchi Motor
A classical example of a highly competitive enterprise in the global market

(*Company profile at a glance*)

Financial data (Fiscal year ended December 1997)

Sales	88,410 (million yen)
Ordinary income	20,839 (million yen)
ROE	7.7%
No. of employees	945

Market share in the world (estimate)

Small DC motors	50%+

1) 50% share of the small DC motor market worldwide

Mabuchi Motor has a share exceeding 50% of the small motor market worldwide. Their small motors are widely used in audio and visual equipment such as VTRs and CD players, electric components for automobiles such as car mirrors and power windows, tools and precision machines such as electric drills and copying machines, and toys and models such as model cars and RC vehicles. Their total production exceeds 1.4 billion motors and more than 100 of their

Chart 4-1 Mabuchi Group Network

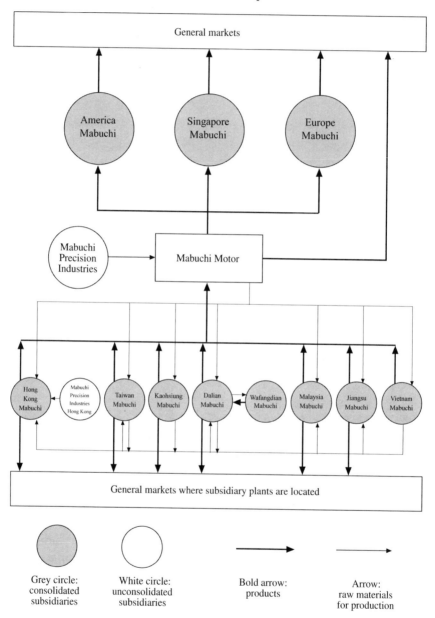

(Source: Mabuchi Motor Comprehensive Financial Statements, December 1997, p. 59)

products have set world standards. All of their small motors are manufactured overseas.

2) High-quality low-cost products by division of labor on a
   global scale

Ryuichi Mabuchi, president of Mabuchi Motor, believes that being
the lowest cost producer in the world is the prerequisite for becoming
the best in the market. Since the founding of the company he has looked
at his company's competitiveness on a global scale. Low price, however,
is not the only reason why Mabuchi Motor has become a "Top Global
Company". Placing technical competence, cost-competitiveness, and
sales power on an equal footing, on the one hand, and achieving high
quality and low cost simultaneously, on the other, are the secret of their
success.

Mabuchi concentrates all of their management resources on their
niche specialty of small motors. They are not interested in diversification
for fear of resource dispersion. Their asset is the systematic technology
and know-how embedded in basic research, product development,
product designing, and production technology. It is what pulls them
away from their competitors. Their refined technology is the fruit of
specialization and focus.

Mabuchi's high-quality low-cost products are manufactured and
marketed by division of labor on a global scale. In this system, the head
office only undertakes R&D, marketing, technical service, and the
management of the overseas subsidiaries. Mabuchi's small motors are all
manufactured by overseas subsidiaries.

Plant locations are selected from a global point of view. They
strategically build their plants where labor is available at the lowest cost.
This classical approach to transplanting is the source of the outstanding
cost competitiveness of the company.

Mabuchi's transplanting started in 1964, when they built a factory in
Hong Kong. This was followed by factories in Taiwan, China, Malaysia
and Vietnam. At any time, approximately 60 experts in production

technology are stationed in these factories. In addition, engineers of the main office make frequent visits to their factories located in Asia. The newest technology and know-how developed in Japan is immediately transferred to their factories in Asia to permit them to manufacture high-quality products without delay. They have built a powerful sales network around the world by connecting their sales offices located in the U.S.A., Germany, Hong Kong, Singapore and China.

With their outstanding technical competence, cost-competitiveness, and sales power, Mabuchi has had more than one hundred of their products accepted as the world standards. This has made Mabuchi, a component manufacturer, powerful enough to influence the direction of product development of their customers: manufacturers of finished products.

3) Ideas and contrivances for minimizing cost

Mabuchi has strived to increase the use of common parts in their products and standardize the latter. This is because product standardization not only contributes to cost minimizing but also permits the company to respond to customers' orders for large quantities at short notice.

Mabuchi develops and fabricates their own production equipment rather than buy it from vendors, because they know in-house equipment is much cheaper. They also pay for capital investment out of their own reserve to avoid resultant interest payment rather than borrow money.

The staff in the headquarters is also expected to raise its cost consciousness. People engaged in the administrative and R&D functions are trained to check their own productivity by comparing it with the cost of outsourcing estimated by outside vendors. This is to arouse a sense of urgency in employees and make them contrive ways to improve their productivity. Those who cannot do so cannot survive in the company.

Manufacturers tend to pay attention only to cost reduction in the factories, but Mabuchi is different. Their cost consciousness is prevalent throughout the organization, encompassing the administrative and R&D

personnel as well, whose productivity is closely monitored. There is much to learn from Mabuchi's thorough cost management in the light of the low productivity of white-collar workers in Japan, which has been a subject of public discussion.

4) "Coexistence and Co-prosperity in Adopted Countries"

Mabuchi's motors are manufactured 100% by their overseas factories. It is not, therefore, an exaggeration to call the management of those factories the lifeline of the company. Under the company motto "Coexistence and Co-prosperity in Adopted Countries", Mabuchi has nurtured long term relationships with the countries where they have built their factories. When they have to move production from one factory in one country to another factory in a different country because of rising labor cost, they do not abandon the original factory. Instead, they transfer advanced technology to that factory and convert it into a base for more sophisticated work. Through this conversion, the original factory can continue to contribute to the economy of the country. An example of this is Mabuchi's factory in Taiwan. It was originally a factory to manufacturer motors. As the labor cost increased with the growth of Taiwan's economy, Mabuchi converted the factory into a designing center for production equipment, and kept its relationship with Taiwan.

Mabuchi is careful enough to adapt the plan for a factory to the situation of the country under consideration. For example, a developing country that has an abundance of labor may not welcome a fully automated factory. Mabuchi then builds a factory in which labor replaces some machines so as to create more job opportunities. Thus, their overseas factories are organized to strike an optimum balance between people and machines.

"Coexistence and Co-prosperity in Adopted Countries" centers on people. According to the company's vision that "capable people are the best asset of the company", Mabuchi trains workers in their overseas factories through on-the-job training and international personnel training programs. The goal is to make them competent by world standards.

In China, Mabuchi pays higher wages to locally hired workers than state enterprises do, and give them opportunities to continue their education. Mabuchi does not hesitate to invest in more than forty-five thousand employees in the world so as to raise their skill and competence. Mabuchi today is a product of its step-by-step effort to become a member of the communities in its adopted countries.

II. Minebea
Production in Asia, sales in Japan, America, and Europe

(*Company profile at a glance*)

Financial data (Fiscal year ended December 1998)

Sales	221,959 (million yen)
Ordinary income	16,631 (million yen)
ROE	3.6%
No. of employees	2,826

Market share in the world (estimate)

Pivot assemblies	70%
Miniature bearings	60%
Rod end bearings for airplanes	60%

1) Top manufacturer of miniature bearings

Minebea has a 60% share of the worldwide market of ball bearings less than 22 mm in external diameter. Main applications of small and miniature bearings include hard disk and CD-ROM drives. They dominate the market of pivot assemblies worldwide. They also have a large market share in rod end bearings for airplanes. Other Minebea products include electronic and machine parts such as FDD sub-assemblies, precision small motors, and switching power units. Ninety percent of their products are manufactured in their overseas factories.

2) Factories all in Asia

The expansion of the market of information equipment such as personal computers has forced manufacturers of bearings to advance their technology in order to manufacture products of higher precision. Furthermore, rapid technical innovation in the information industry requires that bearing manufacturers be able to mass produce what the customers want in a short lead time.

Minebea has built factories in Asia since 1972, when their first overseas factory was built in Singapore. The capability of those factories has been enhanced with the newest equipment. For example, a state-of-the-art clean room was installed in the factory in Thailand, which employs 25,000 people. In 1996, Minebea built the world's largest integrated bearing factory in Shanghai that manufactures miniature bearings.

At present, overseas production amounts to 88% of the total production of the company. As much as 97% of Minebea's miniature bearings is made in Asia. Even their high-tech products such as HDD parts and fan motors that use miniature bearings are manufactured in their integrated factories in Asia.

Minebea's production network in Asia has enabled them to mass-produce high quality products at low cost and have a 60% share of the miniature bearing market worldwide. Such a high market share permits the company to take advantage of the scale of production and makes it difficult for competitors to catch up.

The currency crisis in Asia had a favorable effect on Minebea's strategy to build factories in Asia to manufacture products to be sold in Japan, America and Europe. The decline of local currencies reduced production costs and made Minebea's products more cost competitive in the export market.

3) Karuizawa Plant as home for production worldwide

The secret of Minebea's speedy development and manufacture of products that meet customers' needs is kept in the company's Karuizawa

Plant. As the density of the disks used in personal computers increases, the gap between the disk and the head gets extremely narrow. Such a narrow gap can only tolerate play on the order of 0.1 μm in the bearing that supports the head. High precision bearings for this kind of application are made by Karuizawa Plant.

Karuizawa Plant is the company's center of technology. It performs basic work for high precision bearings, which include materials science, designing, product development, and prototyping. It also takes charge of developing and building production equipment.

The newest equipment made by Karuizawa Plant is shipped to overseas factories. In addition, engineers of Karuizawa Plant visit overseas factories to teach engineers there fine details of know-how that are difficult to communicate by manuals. Engineers of overseas factories in turn visit Karuizawa for training, and learn how to build the production equipment in question by themselves. It is this thorough knowledge of production equipment that makes them experts of precision machining.

Thus, Karuizawa Plant plays the role of the mother plant that unites the company's overseas factories and operation in Japan in terms of both hardware and software.

4) Higher precision to compete with fluid dynamic bearings

Minebea has been the sole winner in the miniature bearing market, but they feel threatened by the advent of fluid dynamic bearing motors. For the widespread use of fluid dynamic bearing motors, which run quieter and last longer than mechanical bearing motors, would deal a grievous blow to the bearing business of Minebea. Minebea's answer to the threat is to produce bearings that promise to deliver higher performance than fluid dynamic bearings. Such bearings require balls of high sphericity. Karuizawa Plant is undertaking a project to develop a technology to achieve a sphericity of 0.05 μm or less. The project aims at improving precision machining technology and the production process, and developing production equipment. The R&D for the project is taking place in a clean room equipped with the newest testing equipment under a soundproof roof.

Contrary to the conventional view that there is not much room left for innovation in the technology of bearings, Minebea is determined to win the technology competition by meeting the challenge of further improving the precision of bearings.

5) Back to the core business

Under the presidency of the late Takami Takahashi, a member of the company founder's family, Minebea actively pursued diversification through aggressive M&A. The newly acquired businesses included semiconductor, drapery, cosmetics, and credit sales, which required business acumen totally different from Minebea's core competence. As a result, those new businesses came to a standstill, accumulating huge interest-bearing debt.

In 1989, Takami Takahashi passed away suddenly, and Goro Ogino became the president. Ogino set out to get rid of unprofitable businesses, and in 1993, he sold the semiconductor business to Nippon Steel. In 1994, the credit sales business was sold to GE Capital (U.S.A.). At the same time, he also set out to restructure Minebea's group companies. As a result, Actus Corporation, a distributor of imported furniture, New Hampshire Ball Bearings, Inc., and Minebea Electronics (UK) Ltd came to report profits.

Thanks to the success in restructuring and the healthy performance of the core business, Minebea recovered and reported the highest operating income in the company's history for the fiscal year ending in March 1998. Interest-bearing debt for the same period decreased to 275 billion yen. By abandoning diversification and concentrating the company's management resources on the core business, Minebea regained its competitiveness.

III. Tokyo Electron
Globalizing human resource to respond to technical innovation

(*Company profile at a glance*)

Financial data (Fiscal year ended March 1998)

Sales	423,752 (million yen)
Ordinary income	51,660 (million yen)
ROE	11.3%
No. of employees	1,265

Market share in the world (estimate)

Diffusion furnaces, CVD equipment	48%
Oxide film etcher	46%

1) Leading company of semiconductor manufacturing equipment

Tokyo Electron is a leading company of semiconductor manufacturing equipment. It has the top market share in diffusion furnaces, CVD equipment, and oxide film etchers. It also manufactures spattering equipment, IC/LSI test systems, assembly equipment, test equipment for wafer processing, and dry etching equipment. They are also a distributor of computer systems such as UNIX server systems, and electronic components such as microprocessors.

2) Reinforcement of personnel overseas for collecting information

Producers of semiconductor manufacturing equipment can survive only if they are capable of collecting information about the future needs of semiconductor companies and developing equipment accordingly. With innovative technologies for MPU and other devices, American semiconductor houses now lead the world in the competition of technological development. Semiconductor equipment producers, therefore, must keep abreast of the developments at American semiconductor houses.

Chart 4-2   Tokyo Electron's Overseas Subsidiaries and Number of Employees

(1998 March 31)

Tokyo Electron America		Number of Employees (Local Employees)
Head Office:	Austin	294 (294)
Branch Offices:	Dallas	46 (42)
	East Fishkill	27 (26)
	Los Angeles	3 (1)
	Manassas	24 (20)
	Phoenix	20 (19)
	Portland	60 (45)
	Richmond	19 (18)
	Roseville	1 (1)
	Santa Clara	53 (41)
	South Portland	4 (4)
Tokyo Electron Oregon		134 (110)
Tokyo Electron Massachusetts		
Head Office:	Beverley	90 (83)
Branch Office:	Santa Clara	22 (4)
Tokyo Electron Texas		57 (46)
Tokyo Electron Arizona		226 (226)
Tokyo Electron Europe		
Head Office:	Crawley (UK)	123 (103)
Branch Offices:	Livingston (UK)	45 (42)
	Newcastle (UK)	10 (10)
Warehouse:	Crawley (UK)	4 (4)
Branch Offices:	Grenoble (France)	14 (14)
	Nijmegen (Netherlands)	14 (13)
Tokyo Electron Korea		
Head Office:	Seongnam	244 (242)
Branch Offices:	Cheongju	5 (5)
	Kumi	1 (1)
	Bucheon	1 (1)
	Icheon	1 (1)
	Kiheung	1 (1)
Training center:	Seongnam	5 (5)
Repair shop:	Seongnam	6 (6)
Control room:	Seongnam	2 (2)
Tokyo Electron Taiwan		47 (39)

(Source: Tokyo Electron Comprehensive Financial Statements, March 1998, p. 26)

Tokyo Electron has reinforced its personnel working in America in order to enhance the company's capability of collecting technical information on American semiconductor houses. The largest increase has been in the number of repair engineers and salespeople. They are stationed near the plants of semiconductor customers. If there is some trouble with the equipment sold to a customer, a repair engineer who is in charge of the customer visits the customer's plant right away. While he is doing repair and maintenance work, he collects technical information of the customer's manufacturing process. Salespeople also strive to probe technical innovations in progress at the customers' plants which they are visiting. Thus, Tokyo Electron's repair engineers and salespeople are expected not only to perform their primary job functions but also to fulfill the important function of gathering information.

In 1994, Tokyo Electron switched from sales through agents to direct sales by their own salespeople. The reason was the need to collect first-hand information from customers so that they might not be left behind in the competition of developing equipment to customers' future needs.

Tokyo Electron is planning to double the current overseas personnel by the Year 2000. Their strategy is to spread their network into growth markets by globalizing their personnel and catching future technology trends in time.

3) Investment in advance in preparation for changes in the market

In order to respond quickly to the changing needs of customers, equipment vendors must be capable of developing and manufacturing products at locations near the customers. Following this wisdom, the company built a plant in Texas in 1998 to manufacture equipment to coat and develop photosensitive emulsion. At the same time, they increased the production capacity of their plants in Oregon and Massachusetts. The company is striving to carve out a substantial share of the US market for their products with their own production facilities, sales force and maintenance service staff. With their characteristic swiftness, they have shifted their focus from the rapidly declining Asian market to the growing US market.

The semiconductor industry advances with rapid technical innovations. Participants in this industry, therefore, have to keep developing new technologies. For this reason, Tokyo Electron invested 9 billion yen to build the Process Technology Center within the premises of their Yamashina factory. The center is to develop next generation semiconductor manufacturing equipment. The center has already started R&D projects for 300 mm silicon wafers, which are expected largely to replace conventional wafers around the year 2000. Strategic investment in advance in preparation for prospective changes in the market has supported the growth of the company.

4) Maintenance service on-line

Semiconductor manufacturing equipment requires delicate tuning and frequent regular maintenance, because its function depends on dimensional control in the order of micrometers. The quality of maintenance service, therefore, is the key to sales promotion. For this reason, Tokyo Electron has increased the number of service centers overseas and hired more repair engineers to improve its maintenance service. It has, however, become difficult to maintain the quality of service only with maintenance engineers, because more customers ask for 24-hour maintenance service now. They have therefore decided to organize a "global (service) network system" to provide customers with on-line information and services such as information of products shipped to customers and manuals for trouble-shooting and repairs. Once completed by the year 2000, the system will enable customers to perform maintenance by themselves simply by following the instructions displayed on the screen of a personal computer. The on-line maintenance service would also benefit the company, since it would reduce the burden of spending time to train service engineers, which is lengthening due to the increasing complexity of the equipment.

5) Discontinuing stable dividend distribution

Tokyo Electron discontinued the traditional dividend policy that stipulates distribution of a stable dividend year after year and replaced it with a new profit sharing policy that links the dividend with the company's performance. Since Japanese companies have taken the traditional stable dividend policy as a golden rule, Tokyo Electron's new policy created a stir.

Some shareholders including life insurance companies still want to receive stable dividends. A majority of shareholders, however, prefer an increase in the stock price to a stable dividend. When the company performance dropped in the fiscal year ended March 1999, Tokyo Electron decided to reduce the annual dividend from 30 yen per share to 12 yen per share. They did not hear many complaints from shareholders when the decision was announced. One of the reasons for the support of the new policy by shareholders is the high ratio (about 30%) of shares owned by foreign investors to the total number of shares.

In 1995, the company introduced an incentive plan for the company's directors and staff. According to the plan, the directors and staff receive special compensation linked to the performance of the company. Since the compensation is determined by the incremental increase in the stock price, capital gain becomes an incentive to directors and staff to work for the company goal of a higher stock price. Linking the dividend to be paid to the shareholders with company performance is based on the same idea. Tokyo Electron's profit sharing system to link the dividend and compensation with company performance is expected to cause a change in the traditional management style in Japan.

Chapter Five

First in the World

I. Yupo Corporation
Synthetic paper Yupo and its ingenious applications in the global market

(Company profile at a glance)

Financial data (Fiscal year ended March 1998)

Sales	16,407 (million yen)
Declared income	2,788 (million yen)
No. of employees	330

Worldwide market share (estimate)

Synthetic paper	80%

1) 80% market share in synthetic paper

The consumption of paper increased drastically in the latter half of the 1960s. The Japanese government was alarmed by this, and to conserve forestry resources, urged the industry to develop oil-based synthetic papers. Oji Paper and Mitsubishi Petrochemical Company (now Mitsubishi Chemical Corporation) responded to this call and formed Yupo Corporation to commercialize synthetic papers. The company developed Yupo, the first synthetic paper in the world. The paper has many advantages over natural papers. By aggressively developing the applications of the paper, Yupo Corporation became a *Top Global Company* with an 80% worldwide market share in synthetic papers.

2) Applications for making the most use of synthetic paper

Developing new technology or products for the first time in the world does not automatically make a company a *Top Global Company*. The challenge is to find applications and markets for the new technology and products.

The synthetic paper Yupo is made of polypropylene resins, inorganic fillers, and additives. This results in certain characteristics that differentiate it from natural papers. As demonstrated by the examples listed below, Yupo Corporation has explored and developed applications that make the most of those characteristics.

Yupo Corporation found outdoor posters and banners for Yupo's excellent resistance against water and sunshine, and took that application from natural papers. The printability and tear resistance helped open the market of maps and labels put on groceries.

The synthetic paper generates little dust. Good use was then made of this property in clean rooms of semiconductor plants, and the demand grew in the 1980s. It also came to be used as paper for copier machines and printers, self-adhesive paper, shopping bags, and heat-sensitive package tags.

Since the latter half of the 1980s, ballots made of the synthetic paper have been used. Being difficult to fold is a defect in the applications where the synthetic paper is expected to behave like a paper. This, however, is a blessing in ballot counting, because ballots made of synthetic paper do not have to be unfolded, and as a result, ballot counting takes less time. This application is a result of "reverse thinking".

In 1994, with the advent of **α-Yupo**, which could be made as thick as 950 μm, the application of synthetic paper expanded to include stereo-maps, stereo-advertisements, and safety signs.

Although it is made from oil, the synthetic paper burns without producing toxic gases. For this reason, its use as an environmentally friendly raw material has increased.

Thus, making the most use of the characteristics of the synthetic paper, Yupo Corporation has found ingenious applications and developed the market throughout the world.

3) Transforming adversity into opportunity

In 1973, four years after it was founded, Yupo Corporation was confronted by the oil crisis. A sudden rise in the price of oil made the synthetic paper more costly than natural paper. By that time, more than twenty companies from the paper, synthetic textile, and chemical industries had entered into the synthetic paper market. In the face of the oil crisis, however, all of those companies except Yupo Corporation and Nisshin Spinning withdrew from the field.

Yupo Corporation faced up to the adversity and set out to transform it into opportunity. Despite the company's loss for 10 years from 1969, the parent companies did not doubt the future of synthetic paper and continued to support Yupo with people and funds. The withdrawal of competitors helped Yupo to increase its market share. Taking advantage of the situation, Yupo further expanded the market by aggressively exploiting the application of synthetic paper.

Thanks to Yupo's determination, the synthetic paper market expanded, and in the 1990s, it became large enough to attract new competitors including Tokai Pulp and Jujo Paper. The example of Yupo demonstrates the importance of foresight to the success of a company.

4) Global production and sales

In 1994, Yupo Corporation opened a sales office in Hong Kong in response to the surge of orders from South East Asia and China. Main applications of the synthetic paper in Asia include posters, self-adhesive labels, and high-grade business cards.

More than a half of Yupo's exports are shipped to the US market. Kimberley-Clark is the sales agent there. The European market is handled by Yupo's sales office in Brussels. The targeted applications in the European market are functional products such as labels for bottles and heat-sensitive tags used by airlines.

In 1996, a wholly owned subsidiary called Yupo Corporation was founded in Chesapeake, Virginia, and also that year, production started in a new plant of an annual capacity of 10,000 ton. Although the plant was built to meet the increasing demand in the US market, it is intended to be the base to develop markets in Central and South America as well. Thus, Yupo Corporation has continued to manifest its strength in finding market-specific applications of its synthetic paper.

II. Disco Corporation
"No. 1 Company" carved out of a traditional business

(*Company profile at a glance*)

Financial data (Fiscal year ended March 1998)

Sales	31,580 (million yen)
Ordinary income	5,840 (million yen)
ROE	11.3%
No. of employees	868

Market share in the world (estimate)

Grinding and cutting machines for semiconductors 70%

1) Top manufacturer of dicing/cutting saws for semiconductors

Disco Corporation has a 70% market share worldwide and 90% share of the domestic market, respectively, in dicing/cutting saws for semiconductors. Also manufacturing cutting and grinding machines for construction industries and diamond tools for stone, Disco is the top manufacturer of cutting and grinding machinery. Disco is in a class of its own in that, through its own innovation, it has carved its specialization in precision cutting out of the traditional grinding wheel business.

2) Specializing in cutting with thin grinding wheels

Disco was founded as Dai-ichi Seitosha in 1937, with its headquarters located in Kure (Hiroshima Prefecture). It was an innovative company even in the early days; it was the first company in Japan to use recycled materials for grinding wheels. The company moved to Tokyo in 1940, not only for facilitating sales but also for collecting the newest information on customers and technology. It was the customers' suggestion of a promising future of precision grinding wheels that prompted Disco to start developing thin grinding wheels. The development resulted in reinforced, resinoid-bonded thin grinding wheels that could be used for cutting. Their production started in 1942. Disco had also developed the technological know-how of using thin grinding wheels for cutting, which later permitted Disco to make a big leap.

The end of the Second World War brought a construction boom in Japan. More houses meant more watt-hour meters, which meant more cut-off wheels to make a cut in C-shaped magnets used in watt-hour meters. In response to this demand, Disco developed a cut-off wheel of 1.2 mm thickness and sold them to the manufacturers of watt-hour meters.

In 1956, an ultra-thin cut-off wheel with a thickness of 140 µm was developed to slit the nibs of fountain pens. Disco continued to strive to develop thinner wheels, and succeeded in developing precision cut-off wheels that could be used to slice and cut electronic parts. In 1964, Disco decided to discontinue the production of vitrified grinding wheels and concentrate on ultra-thin resinoid-bonded cut-off wheels. It was a turning point to redirect the company's business from grinding to cutting.

3) Ultra-thin cut-off wheels for the semiconductor industry

In 1968, Disco developed an ultra-thin cut-off wheel called "Microncut" with a thickness of 40 μm. Thanks to the diamond powder contained in the wheel, "Microncut" was capable of making such sharp, precision cuts as demanded in the semiconductor manufacturing process.

Many inquiries came from semiconductor manufacturers, but they did not result in sales. This was because there were no cutting machines available in the market on which the ultra-thin precision cut-off wheel could be mounted and run. Disco therefore decided to develop its own cutting machine for "Microncut". After much trial and error, the first successful model, the DAD-2H, was completed in 1975. When presented at an exhibition in America, the cutting machine was given instantaneous recognition by many American semiconductor houses including Texas Instruments. A surge of orders followed, which then prompted Japanese semiconductor houses to adopt DAD-2H.

A fully automated cutting machine, DAD-2HS, was introduced into the market in 1978 and Series 650, the newest model, in 1980. In 1977, the company shed its skin by changing its name from Dai-ichi Seitosha to Disco to become a specialized company in semiconductor cutting machines.

4) Market expansion with user-friendly machines

It is largely due to ingenious marketing strategies that Disco, an obscure grinding wheel manufacturer, became a *Top Global Company*. Disco realized that an ultra-thin cut-off wheel could not cut by itself, unless an appropriate cutting machine was developed. They also realized that they had to develop cutting know-how that would help customers use the machine properly and effectively. Based on this realization, Disco has developed its own wheels, cutting machines, and cutting know-how, which are packaged together for customers' convenience. No other company does that in this field.

Since different semiconductors have to be cut differently, it is an important step for Disco's salespeople to learn from customers the detail of cutting jobs to be performed. Based on this information obtained by salespeople, the company then develops specific hardware and software to meet the customers' needs. They also spend time teaching each of their customers how to optimize the cutting conditions such as wheel revolution and cooling method for the specific cutting machine and cutting job. Thus, they give their full attention to the needs and satisfaction of their customers. It is an excellent marketing strategy to provide customers with not only hardware but also software that adds user-friendliness to the hardware.

5) Innovation by using external resources

When Disco decided to develop their own cutting machines, they had neither the facility to manufacture machine tools nor people who had the expertise. A decision was therefore made that Disco only design and assemble, and that the production of the parts be contracted out. This was a viable option because the Ota District of Tokyo, where their headquarters is located, was home to many small job firms which had expertise in manufacturing the parts Disco needed. Were it not for the cooperation of these shops, Disco's cutting machine would not have been born.

The top management of Disco did not have technical background. For this very reason, Disco was eager to collect technical information. Their staff attended many meetings outside the company and gained knowledge and information there. They also actively sought the help of universities and ran joint R&D projects with them. The powerful stimulation they received from external resources enabled them to shed the skin of the traditional grinding wheel industry. Disco's history demonstrates that the effective use of external resources can give birth to unexpected innovations.

III. Horiba
Work with "Joy and Fun", become No. 1

(*Company profile at a glance*)

Financial data (Fiscal year ended March 1998)

Sales	29,443 (million yen)
Ordinary income	2,225 (million yen)
ROE	2.9%
No. of employees	1,074

Worldwide market share (estimate)

Engine emission analyzers	80%

1) 80% worldwide market share in engine emission analyzers

Horiba is a multinational company of measuring instruments. Their products include engine emission analyzers such as automotive emission and CO/HC analyzers, analytical instruments such as pH meters and particle size distribution analyzers, environmental and medical instruments such as air pollution monitors and automatic blood cell counters, and electronic and information instruments such as impurity analyzers for semiconductors and infrared sensors. Horiba has an 80% worldwide market share in engine emission analyzers.

2) Horiba's precept "Joy and Fun"

"Joy and Fun" is Horiba's precept. Horiba's new head office built in the city of Kyoto is called "Joy and Fun Pavilion". Masao Horiba, the founder of the company, is known as a pioneer of student entrepreneurs. It is his unique management philosophy that has shaped the company into a small but powerful brain center. Regarding the relationship between companies and workers, Masao Horiba has a unique idea:

The workplace is where we spend the majority of our life. Companies therefore should provide their workers with environments where workers can achieve self-realization and fulfilling lives. By doing so, companies can transform the workplace into a place where workers are able to work with "joy and fun". Statistics show that if we take interest in our work, our work efficiency improves considerably. If we work with "joy and fun", our productivity increases, which benefits shareholders as well as workers and the company.

We would not be able to survive in the future society, unless we nurture a special ability and individuality that would permit us to do things other people cannot. By the same token, companies would not be able to grow unless they gather such people. Managers and leaders of a company should be able to direct workers as a director directs actors and actresses in a play and bring out the best individuality in workers. We should remember that individuals are not the product of organizations, but that organizations are the product of individuals.

For a company to become a fun and joyful place for workers, profits should be distributed in a reasonable, just, and fair way. In Horiba, salaries and bonuses are determined by the value-added for the fiscal year. Directors' bonuses and the dividend to shareholders are determined by the net income for the fiscal year; a prescribed percentage is not used to determine the dividend. Since its listing, Horiba has fulfilled its pledge to keep the dividend payout ratio at 30%.

3) How the European market was won in emission analyzers

Environmentally conscious Europe is a highly competitive market for the manufacturers of emission gas analyzers. Competing in this market are Siemens and other leading companies. Then, how could Horiba come to have a large market share there?

Developing environmental instruments for the European market requires thorough knowledge of the standards for emission control and local content in each country, because they differ from country to country. Before developing a product for Europe, therefore, Horiba invites European engineers who are knowledgeable about local situations to the head office in Kyoto to join a product development team. Capable Japanese and American engineers are also asked to join the team. The members of the team work together from the product designing stage. At the last stage of product development, Horiba Europe located in Germany takes charge of the fine-tuning to adapt the product to customers' specifications. Horiba's MEXA Series was developed this way. It became a hit, and its universal specifications have become the world standard.

Horiba has spread a professional service network throughout Europe to provide customers with a thorough maintenance service. The high quality of its emission gas analyzers and well-organized maintenance service permitted Horiba to dominate the highly competitive Europe in emission gas analyzers.

This success, however, is not without concern. Since Horiba already has a large market share in emission gas analyzers, growth in sales is prone to slow down in the future. In order to overcome this, Horiba is planning to promote gas-analyzing systems that include engineering services as well as gas analyzing units. This is to sell value-added products and reduce the customers' burden of building their own emission gas analyzing systems with separately purchased measuring instruments.

4) Product development in close contact with customers
    via the Internet

Rapid technological innovation takes place in the industry Horiba is in, and therefore speedy product development is a must. Developing products fast, however, is not enough by itself; the products developed have to meet the customers' needs. An experimental program Horiba started on the Internet has drawn the attention of the industry. It is a program in which customers are invited to participate in Horiba's product development via the Internet.

In October 1997, Horiba's website presented a new section called Advanced Business Collaboration or ABC. It introduces a new product under development with their specifications. Customers can ask questions or express opinions on the page. They can also exchange ideas and opinions with other customers. In the early stage of the product development, customers are asked about product specifications and level of performance they desire. At a later stage of the development, new specifications and performance data are disclosed, and customers' criticism is solicited again. This collaboration, the unique feature of the "ABC" system, continues throughout a product development project, making it a joint project between the manufacturer and customers.

The ABC system gives Horiba the advantage, most of all, of shortening the time to develop a product that meets customers' needs. In addition, customers' advice can lead Horiba's engineers to look into applications of the product they have not been aware of. It is possible that, because of its many advantages, joint product development with customers via the Internet may be widely adopted in the high-tech industries.

5) Reverse landing that helped an obscure company

At the end of the 1960s, Horiba developed an emission gas analyzer and tried to sell it to automakers in Japan. Those companies, however, did not take the then obscure Horiba seriously. They could not entrust an instrument made by such a small unknown company to measure the performance of their engines that are the hearts of their cars, they said. What confronted Horiba was the general mistrust of small, obscure vendors, which is prevalent among Japanese companies. Horiba, therefore, was forced to continue their sales promotion somewhere else. They chose America.

Horiba's obscurity was not a problem in America. American customers recognized their products, not for the name but for their high quality. As Horiba's products gained wide acceptance, Japanese automakers began to buy products from Horiba. Thus, Horiba overcame the weakness of being obscure by reverse landing, namely, landing in the Japanese market from outside Japan with their success in the US market.

6) Road to becoming a great medium-sized company

As the world is becoming more borderless, more severe competition is taking place in the global market. Horiba has become a successful medium-sized company of marked individuality, but faces a new issue. It is expensive to develop analytical and measuring instruments on the leading edge of technology. Horiba estimates that the sales of the Horiba group must reach 100 billion yen or more in year 2000, if it were to survive in the competition of technological innovation. The issue is how to expand the scale of operation without losing the virtue of a venture company.

Horiba has chosen diversification as a means to increase sales. In 1996, they spent 3 billion yen to acquire ABX, a French manufacturer of blood cell counters. Horiba plans to use ABX's medical technology to enter the market of medical instruments. The acquisition of ABX marks Horiba's departure from its "debtless management" which it had followed for a long time.

Atsushi Horiba, the current president of Horiba, said in an interview with a newspaper that his goal is to make the company a great medium-sized company, neither a sluggish big company nor a vulnerable medium-sized company. Horiba is standing at the critical juncture of the road to becoming a great medium-sized company.

Chapter Six

Growing in the Parent Company's Nest

I. Canon Kasei
Standing close to Canon

(*Company profile at a glance*)

Financial data (Fiscal year ended December 1997)

Sales	160,072 (million yen)
Ordinary income	4,245 (million yen)
ROE	9.6%
No. of employees	1,216

Worldwide market share (estimate)

Toner cartridges for laser printers	70%

1) Canon is the customer

Canon Kasei has a 70% worldwide market share in toner cartridges for laser printers. Of its sales, 95% is shipped to Canon, its parent company, which in turn resells on an OEM basis 70% of what is received from Canon Kasei. The company is one of those typical subsidiaries whose sales are closely tied with those of their parent companies' products. As part of product diversification, the company also manufactures rubber parts used for the keys of printing and copying machines.

2) Growing into global No. 1 with the growth of parent company

Canon Kasei was formerly Sanei Industries, a manufacturer and supplier of exposure meters for cameras. In 1980, Sanei Industries became a wholly owned subsidiary of Canon. It now manufactures toner cartridges for laser printers and sells most of them to its captive customer Canon. As Canon gained a large worldwide market share in printers, Canon Kasei became a *Top Global Company*. The two companies share the same destiny.

Canon has been performing very well. The fiscal year that ended in December 1997 was the fourth year in a row that sales and profit increased and the second year in a row that profit was the highest in the company's history. Canon has gained a large share of the laser printer market by covering both ends of the consumer spectrum; it has offered economy models to home users and high speed, high performance models to office users.

The sales of Canon Kasei grew as those of Canon's printers grew. As printing in offices increased, Canon Kasei's sales grew further. Increases in color printing in offices are expected to boost the sales still further. The continuous entry of new competitors into the printer market, however, is forcing the printer manufacturers to compete harder. The issue is how a subsidiary company like Canon Kasei manages its business when the sales of its parent company stagnate.

3) Optimum production system

When the yen strengthened in the latter half of the 1980s, many domestic manufacturers started offshore production. When the value of the yen stabilized, however, some of those companies began to shift their production back to Japan. On the other hand, Canon Kasei reformed its domestic plants, so that they became more cost-competitive than plants overseas. This reformation has drawn attention as a pioneering effort to bring production back to Japan.

At the plants of the company toner cartridges are assembled in two lines, one for manual assembly and the other for automated assembly. The manual line is manned with contract workers. The productivity of the automated line is much higher than that of the manual line, because the number of people for the former is less than one-tenth that for the latter. The manual line, however, is far more flexible and can be adjusted to changes in production volume or kinds of products to manufacture. It is therefore an indispensable part of the reformed production system for higher productivity. The half-automated assembly system of the company has proved to be an optimum production system.

Canon Kasei's Iwama Plant is an integrated plant to manufacture both main parts and final products. Costs associated with purchasing such as handling charges, transportation cost and inspection cost are eliminated by making parts within the plant. As a result of vigorous cost reduction, the Iwama Plant has reportedly become more cost-competitive than plants in China where labor is available at lower cost.

It has been a general trend that, in view of the strength of the yen and high labor cost, Japanese manufacturers move their production facilities to offshore locations. The successful example of Canon Kasei, however, would cause some manufacturers to review their decision criteria for plant locations.

4) Product diversification

In order to overcome the weakness of being highly dependant on the parent company, Canon Kasei is diversifying its line of products. They built an R&D center in Tsukuba in the fall of 1997 as part of their effort to strengthen their product development capability. The number of engineers working in the center is 40 now, but will be increased to 70 in year 2000. The plan is to develop their own products including rubber parts for the keys of printing and copying machines and sell them within and outside the Canon group of companies.

Developing its own products enables a subsidiary company to increase the stock of its own technology. Strengthening R&D, however, is not sufficient for the success of its diversification. Its sales force, a common weakness among subsidiary companies whose captive customers are their parent companies, has to be strengthened in order to develop new customers.

II. Denso
Growing out of the parent company's nest

(*Company profile at a glance*)

Financial data (Fiscal year ended December 1997)

Sales	1,375,133 (million yen)
Ordinary income	85,166 (million yen)
ROE	5.5%
No. of employees	39,390

Worldwide market share (estimate)

Car air conditioners	20%
Car heaters	20%
Alternators	20%
Starter motors	20%

1) Leading the global market in 14 automobile parts

Denso is a leading manufacturer of automobile parts worldwide. They have a top market share in 14 automobile parts, which are listed below:

- Car air conditioners
- Car heaters
- Starters
- Alternators
- Meters for automobiles
- Fuel pumps
- Bus air conditioners
- Compressors for car air conditioners

- Relays for automobiles
- Wiper motors
- Washer motors
- Window motors
- In-vehicle telephones
- Bar code handy terminals (CCD type)

Although automobile components and parts occupy more than 80% of their sales, they have entered new territories such as telecommunications, environmental protection, electronic appliances, factory automation and LCD. About 50% of their sales goes to Toyota Motors, their parent company, which manifests their great dependence on Toyota.

2) Accumulating technology by supporting Toyota Motors

In 1949, Denso was separated from Toyota Motors and became a subsidiary of the latter. They grew with Toyota Motors and became a global manufacturer of automobile parts. The main products are high quality, low cost electric and electronic parts made to Toyota Motor's specifications. Adhering to the Toyota Production System, they pursued strict quality control, and as a result, they were awarded the Deming Prize in 1961.

An automobile parts manufacturer must be able to synchronize its product development with the model change cycle of its customers. Denso, therefore, allocates more than 20% of its work force to R&D to perform a wide range of both basic and applied research. This has enabled them to have a top market share worldwide in as many as 14 items that they have developed. The technology developed for automotive parts has also been used as leverage to enter new territories such as telecommunications equipment and electronic appliances.

In the spring of 1998, Toyota Motor started to construct an online network that would connect eight parts manufacturers in the Toyota group. The network is built on the information recording technology developed by Denso. The idea is to transform the order entry-execution system through the circulation of cards called "Kanban" into an electronic Kanban system so as to significantly shorten the time between order entries to shipping. Once completed, the online network will have converted Toyota's Kanban System into a Kanban-less system.

Having grown into a global manufacturer of automobile parts in the nest of Toyota, Denso is now ready to leap into new businesses.

3) Overcoming economic crisis by following Toyota's lead

The crisis in the Southeast Asian economy that occurred in 1997 has affected Denso's overseas strategies. Their subsidiary plants in Thailand, the Philippines, Indonesia and Malaysia have all been affected. Despite the effort to increase local procurement and reduce expense, it is difficult to expect quick recovery of those plants. They therefore have started to shift their production to North America and other regions where stable market growth is expected.

In North America, they are going to increase the production capacities of their Tennessee and Canadian plants for fuel injection parts, alternators, and air conditioners. This is in response to Toyota's production expansion plan in North America. In India, they are planning to build a factory in 1999 to manufacture car air conditioners and engines for a Toyota's joint venture and other automotive companies.

In contrast to many manufacturers who have not been able to recover from the economic chaos in Southeast Asia, Denso has managed to minimize the damage by shifting its production to promising market regions. They have been able to do so because of their privilege of having Toyota, a global enterprise, as their parent company.

4) Growing out of "Keiretsu"

The automobile industries in the world are undergoing M&A across the borders. M&A is also taking place among automotive parts manufacturers, which results in the collapse of the traditional industrial grouping called "Keiretsu". In the light of this, Denso is searching for a new direction to grow out of Toyota's nest, while taking advantage of its close ties to Toyota.

Denso Manufacturing UK LTD, which is located in the city of Telford, supplies their products not only to Toyota UK but also to Rover, Audi, Volvo, Daimler-Benz and BMW. They are also trying to become a supplier to Volkswagen. In Hungary, Denso has built a plant to manufacture fuel pumps for diesel car manufacturers in Europe.

European automobile manufacturers, Volkswagen and Daimler-Benz, in particular, are shifting their car assembly process from parts-based assembly to module-based assembly. Building cars from modules, in which a number of parts have been pre-assembled, simplifies the assembly process and therefore makes it more efficient and less costly.

Module-based car assembly, which is becoming a worldwide trend, forces automobile parts manufactures to reorganize themselves. Competition in product development among them is getting fierce so much so that companies that cannot compete in quality, price, and technology for designing and building modules will be pushed out of the competition. Denso is aware that such fierce competition will threaten its survival if it keeps managing the company by relying on "Keiretsu" as before. The issue is how to grow out of Toyota's nest.

5) Expansion of the business territory

As the domestic automobile production remains stagnant, Denso is striving to expand its business territory. A considerable effort has been put into the development of ITS (Intelligent Transportation System) business, car navigation systems in particular. Their scope of the future business ranges from in-vehicle instruments to system control. According to their blueprint, their ITS business will grow to occupy 10% of the total sales by the year 2005.

The company's new business in transportation, environmental protection, electronic appliances, factory automation, and LCD has grown considerably in the past few years, the annual sales reaching 100 billion yen. Growth is expected in cell phones, in vehicle hand-free units, and PHS (Personal Handy-phone System) for offices. Environmental business, such as garbage treatment machines, has a great potential for growth as the society is becoming more conscious of environmental protection.

All the new businesses, however, have not turned a profit yet. In contrast to their strength in technology, their sales force is weak which is typical of a company that has grown in the nest of its parent company. In order to be successful in the new businesses, Denso must shed the old skin and become as strong in sales as in technology.

6) Changing corporate culture

In order to win the fierce competition for survival, Denso formulated a new human resource management plan called "Action 21", and has already implemented part of it. The aim of the plan is to change the company's conservative culture that has been nurtured in the parent company's nest.

In 1998, the company started an open recruiting system, in which its employees can apply to the job offers for R&D, designing, and new business posted on the intranet. It also opened the way for a switch from a general clerical job to a main career track. These new systems are aimed at activating the organization.

The company has also made changes in the seniority-based wage system. Managers and higher ranks are now subjected to ability rating, the result of which greatly affects their salary. Furthermore, the assistant managers in nine divisions including the R&D division can now choose an achievement-based wage option, in which one's salary is determined by one's achievement but not by the working hours.

In response to the advancement of globalization, the company has decided to integrate its operations worldwide into a consolidated management system by year 2000. An urgent issue is to train a sufficient number of people who can lead the effort at the company's subsidiaries and plants overseas. Recognizing that the company's conservative culture is a barrier, the company has emphasized in its management climate reformation the importance of nurturing able people through training.

III. Nihon Electric Glass
Independent-minded subsidiary

(Company profile at a glance)

Financial data (Fiscal year ended March 1998)

Sales	228,604 (million yen)
Ordinary income	7,277 (million yen)
ROE	5.5%
No. of employees	3,971

Worldwide market share (estimate)

Cathode-ray tube glass	30%

1) Top manufacturer of cathode-ray tube glass

Nippon Electric Glass holds a 30% worldwide market share in cathode-ray tube glass for black-and-white televisions, color televisions and displays. They also manufacture a variety of glass products including glass tubing, glass for construction and home use, glass for electronic components, and fiberglass.

They have kept the head office in the city of Otsu (Shiga Prefecture) following the parent company's policy that subsidiaries be located where high quality labor is readily available. They have four plants overseas to serve customers worldwide.

2) Success with independent-minded management

In 1949, Nippon Electric Glass was separated from NEC as its subsidiary. Although NEC still holds 42% of its shares, the company has maintained a high degree of independence from NEC. NEC calls its subsidiaries its "alter egos", regarding them as its partners. For this

Chart 6-1   Business Affiliations of Nippon Electric Glass

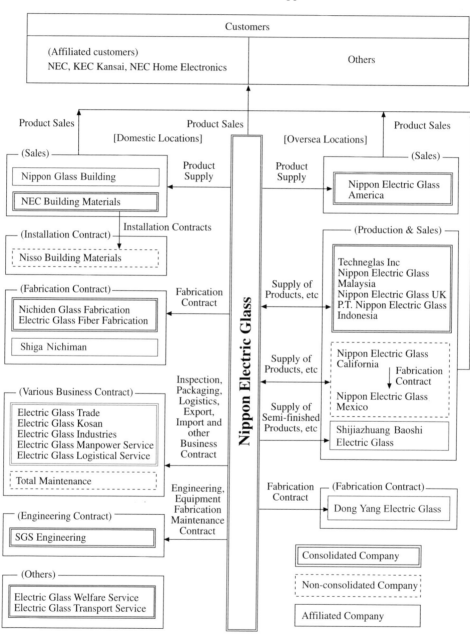

(Source: Nippon Electric Glass Comprehensive Financial Statements, March 1998, p. 55)

reason, many of NEC's subsidiaries are managed largely independent of NEC, and Nippon Electric Glass is one of those independent-minded subsidiaries.

The company has benefited from active exchange of personnel with NEC to increase the skill of its employees. Thus, they have been taking advantage of being a part of the NEC group to advance their expertise in glass. On the other hand, their capability to develop new products one after another and undaunted investment in growth areas mark their stance as an independent-minded specialty glass manufacturer. They have not only acquired technology from the parent company and foreign companies but also developed their own technology. The undaunted investment, in particular, differentiates the company from a typical subsidiary whose managerial decisions are greatly influenced by its parent company.

In 1991, the company built a dedicated plant in Wakasa (Fukui Prefecture) to manufacture glass panels for LCD. Thanks to this brave decision, which was made in anticipation of an increase in future demand, the plant now produces one-third of the current demand in the domestic market.

As a result of its aggressive investment overseas, its overseas plants now employ as many workers as the domestic plants. Thus, the company has firmly established itself as a global specialty glass manufacturer. It makes a good case for an independent-minded subsidiary of a big company.

3) Scrupulous pursuit of technology

Nippon Electric Glass uses advanced technology at every step of its glass manufacturing process that includes materials designing, melting, forming and fabrication. The company therefore refers to its products "high-tech glass", emphasizing their high quality. Since its foundation, the company has strived to improve its manufacturing technology and equipment. Its scrupulous pursuit of technology has given birth to "high-tech glass".

In the 1950s and 1960s, the company developed glass for fluorescent lamps and syringes, glass raw material for fiberglass, glass blocks for construction, and heat-resistant crystallized glass. It started the production of CRT glass bulbs for black-and-white televisions and those for color televisions in 1965 and 1968, respectively. Since then, they have become the company's main products. Since the 1970s, it has commercialized glass for LCD, crystallized glass for construction, alkali-less glass substrate for TFT LCD, and ferrules made of crystallized glass for optic fiber connectors.

The company anticipates market growth for its glass for electronic components and fiberglass. In 1999, it developed a sealing glass for electronic components that can be melted at 280°C, a temperature 40°C lower than the melting point of conventional sealing glasses. Since a multitude of units can be sealed at a time at the lower sealing temperature, the new sealing glass helps increase the productivity of the production of electronic components such as quartz oscillators.

In contrast to the conservative disposition of subsidiary companies in general, the company has energetically developed its own products. Were it not for the enterprising and independent spirit of an alter ego of a big company, the company would not have become a leading manufacturer in the world.

4) Global division of labor in response to regional needs

Global division of labor is the basis for the company's production organization. Its subsidiary plants in the US, UK, Malaysia and Indonesia are manufacturing products to satisfy regional needs. For example, the plant in the US manufactures CRT glass bulbs for desktop computers and large televisions, and the plants in Southeast Asia CRT glass bulbs for televisions and glass for lighting.

The domestic plants mainly manufacture value-added, leading-edge products such as LCD glass, fiberglass and glass for PDP (Plasma Display Panel). The company has plans to build plants in China and Mexico to meet increasing demand for CRT bulbs for televisions.

The efficient division of labor among the company's five regional production bases including the one in Japan has strengthened its resistance against exchange rate fluctuation and increased its global competitiveness.

5) Technology for recycling CRT glass

The law called the Management System for Used Home Appliances becomes effective in year 2001. The front glass of CRT is difficult to recycle because the refuse contains a variety of glass compositions and colors which cannot be reused as a raw material to produce new batches of CRT front glass to tight specifications.

In the light of its annual production of 45 million sets of CRT bulbs, Nippon Electric Glass tackled the tough challenges presented by forthcoming legislation and succeeded in developing a recycling process for CRT front glass. Their solution was to finely crush recycled pieces of used glass and then remove metallic impurities. The new process made it possible to recycle the total amount of used CRT glass disposed every year.

The forthcoming legislation has the effect of eliminating non-recyclable products from the market. The newly developed recycling technology gives Nippon Electric Glass a competitive edge over its rivals and puts its products ahead of others.

Chapter Seven

Creating New Business

1) Distribution chain of high earning power and its information system support

Take a look at a typical chain store of Seven-Eleven Japan and you'll find 3,000 fast-selling articles displayed in a floor area of 300 m². The average daily sales of such a store are far more than those of competing stores, reaching almost 7 hundred thousand yen. In the fiscal year that ended in February 1998, the total sales of the whole chain exceeded

Chart 7-1   Comparison of the Ordinary Income of Distributors

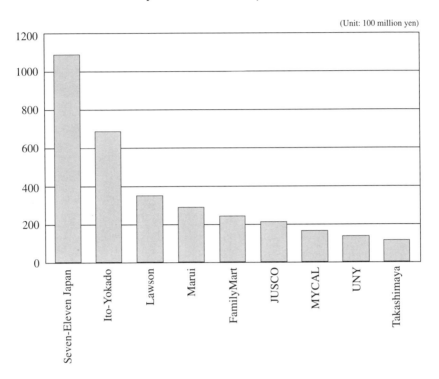

(Unit: 100 million yen)

1,700 billion yen or a little more than 30% of the total sales by convenience stores in Japan. The company's ordinary income, which exceeds 110 billion yen, places it at the top among the distributors. A superb POS (Point-of-Sales) system is used to keep track of each of the articles sold. The system is regarded as world standard.

2) Creating a new style of business in response to a change in society

In 1973, Ito-Yokado Co., Ltd. founded Seven-Eleven Japan to start a convenience store business. Convenience stores, a new style of retail business, were created to satisfy a new need of consumers.

Japan in the 1970s was no longer a poor country. The living standard became higher and the active hours of the day longer. Richer and busier, consumers began to look for "convenience" more than a "bargain". This new need could not be met either by large supermarkets or by small and medium-sized retailers, because it was their bargain prices that had helped them to grow rapidly in the 1960s.

Seven-Eleven Japan provided consumers with four kinds of convenience stores to meet the diverse needs of consumers living in prosperous times. They were "convenience stores for time-convenience", which are open even on holidays and in the evenings, "convenience stores for distance-convenience", which are located near train stations and in residential areas, "convenience stores for one-stop shopping", where you can buy everything you need, and "convenience stores for quick shopping", for easy and quick shopping.

3) Expansion of the chain through franchising

Retailers underwent great changes in the 1970s. Many small and medium-sized retailers including those located around train stations found it difficult to keep their stores open. They lacked successors of their business and were losing business to large supermarkets. For protecting those retailers, the government enforced the Large-Scale Retail Stores Law in 1974. It put strict limitations on large stores in the shopping districts located, for example, around train stations. Supermarkets then built large stores with parking lots in the suburbs and pulled customers away from small and medium-size stores, which had become complacent and still less competitive under the protection of the law.

When it became difficult to open large stores in the shopping districts, Ito-Yokado decided to concentrate on small stores, and for this purpose, founded Seven-Eleven Japan. The average floor area of their stores was set at 300 m^2, in compliance with the law.

Out of the concern that making their stores smaller may not be enough to gain the acceptance of local retailers, Seven-Eleven decided to expand the chain through the sale of franchises to those retailers whose future were in jeopardy. This policy has helped the company to multiply affiliated stores incredibly fast. There are now more than 7,400 stores affiliated with the chain around the country.

4) Information system — the secret of strength

Seven-Eleven Japan has built an extensive information system that connects the head office, affiliated stores, regional offices and clients. It is a multimedia system consisting of seven subsystems, one of which is a POS (Point-of-Sales) information system. Information flows through a satellite channel from the head office to the affiliated stores and through an ISDN channel from the stores to the head office. This system plays a key role in the company's store management, product development and distribution.

The POS system enables real-time tracking of each of the articles sold. Each store strictly adheres to the system to eliminate dead stock. Goods sold at Seven-Eleven stores are fast-selling articles that have been carefully selected. This enables the company to achieve the highest average daily sales per store in the industry. In order to save labor and time, orders are placed with a GOT (Graphic Order Terminal) and the incoming merchandise is inspected with an ST (Scanner Terminal).

Information collected by the POS system is indispensable to product development. It permits the company to quickly develop products that meet the rapidly changing needs of consumers. Seven-Eleven Japan develops new products jointly with large producers. The real-time consumer information gathered from more than 7,400 stores is extremely valuable to those producers, because they themselves do not have channels to make direct contact with consumers.

The orders placed by a single store are in small batches. Furthermore, merchandise such as fast food that has to be kept fresh must be delivered to each store several times a day. To facilitate frequent delivery of such small batches, the company developed an innovative delivery system called "pooled delivery". In this system, the articles of

Chart 7-2   5th Total Information System of Seven-Eleven

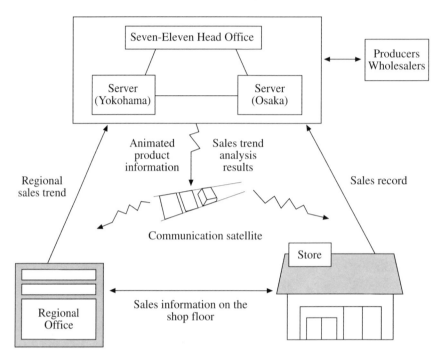

(Source: Nihon Keizai Shimbun, 16 October 1997)

merchandise to be delivered are first deposited at a pooled delivery center. They are then delivered to individual area stores by dedicated delivery cars. Information about orders and inventory is communicated through the company's information system to the pooled delivery centers and the vendors, so that the ordered articles are delivered in time and in specified quantities.

The head office prepares animated product information and sales promotion material for enhancing the sales of the stores. The information system offers a powerful conduit for the head office to communicate those sales enhancement tools to each of its stores. It forms the backbone of the management.

5) Sales expansion based on accurate information of order patterns

The geographical condition and the demography of customers of one store are different from those of another. The company therefore does not prepare a unified set of goods for all the stores but lets each store make its own list of sales items.

POS information, no matter how valuable it may be, is merely a record of the past. It does not tell the stores how tomorrow's sales would be. Each of the affiliated stores, therefore, makes an assumption about tomorrow's sales and uses it to place orders for specific items. The assumption is based on such input as POS statistics, special events scheduled in the area, and weather. Its validity is later examined in comparison with the actual sales. By reiterating the cycle of assumption, execution, and verification, each store improves the accuracy of its order replacement.

Chart 7-3   Services Offered at the Counter of Seven-Eleven Stores

Teller Service	Public utility bills, mail order, insurance, subscription fees, driving school fees, JAF membership fees, correspondence courses
Brokerage	DPE of pictures, door-to-door parcel service, printing of greeting cards, cleaning, driving school registration, regular car inspection, copying
Sales & Booking	Catalog sale, ticket sales, mail stamps, postcards, stamp duty, magazine subscriptions, music CDs, videos, game software, prepaid cards
Non-Cash Account Settlement	Prepaid card settlement

Notes: some services offered only at selected stores
(Source: *Nikkei Ryutsu Shimbun*, 9 January 1999)

The company emphasizes that human beings place orders according to their own judgment, and that the information system is just a tool (hardware) to help that human action. The company's incessant effort to improve people's ability (software) is what enables the affiliated stores to increase their sales.

6) Transforming convenience stores beyond retail

Seven-Eleven stores are not just selling goods. Since the latter half of the 1980s, they have provided a variety of services. For example, people now can pay public utility bills and deposit packages for door-to-door delivery there. Against a backdrop of deregulation, these stores in the future may provide financial services, accept tax payment and sell medicines.

Chains of convenience stores were born in the 1970s as a new style of retail. Their powerful network of a large number of affiliated stores is becoming a part of the infrastructure of our society. In the 21st century, these chains may be transformed into a yet new style of business beyond retail.

II. Yamato Transport
Defying the conventional wisdom of the transport industry

(*Company profile at a glance*)

Financial data (Fiscal year ended March 1998)
Sales	690,590 (million yen)
Ordinary income	26,644 (million yen)
ROE	5.1%
No. of employees	74,193

Domestic market share (estimate)
Door-to-door parcel delivery service	46.6%

1) Paramount leader in door-to-door parcel delivery service

Yamato Transport has a slightly more than 46% market share in door-to-door parcel delivery service in Japan. The parcel delivery service is called "*Takkyubin*" meaning "door-to-door express parcel delivery service". Its 1,800 sales offices are located all around the country from Hokkaido to Okinawa. The total volume of *Takkyubin* exceeds 700 million a year. Its *Cool Takkyubin* service in refrigerator-freezer vans has pulled itself ahead of the competition. Other services of the company include *Ski Takkyubin, Golf Takkyubin, Book Service, Collect Service* and *Kuroneko Mail Service*. The company has also entered into domestic transport, international transport, information and telecommunications services, logistic services and products retail.

2) How *Takkyubin* was born

Yamato Transport, which gave birth to *Takkyubin* in 1971, has a long history. It was founded in 1919 for the business of transporting goods by truck. Mitsukoshi department store was one of its major clients. In 1929, following the model of Carter Paterson's parcel collection-delivery system, it started a route transport between Tokyo and Yokohama. The present *Takkyubin* may have its roots in this transport service, which was called *Yamatobin*. The company is commended for its foresight to initiate a transport service to homes at such an early period.

The company's parcel delivery service, however, was put on the back burner in the postwar era of high economic growth. Cargo transport for industrial customers became the major line of business of transport companies, and Yamato Transport was no exception. It dominated the short and middle distance transport market in the Kanto region and became number one in the industry. When the long distance transport market expanded in the 1960s, however, the company missed the opportunity, and as a result, its performance fell. In the 1970s, it was hit by the oil crisis, and its performance deteriorated so much as to cause lay-offs.

In order to ride out the storm, Masao Ogura, then president of the company, decided to shift its business from commercial cargo transport to home parcel delivery. At that time, the conventional wisdom in the industry was that money could not be made on a parcel delivery service because collecting and delivering small packages would be too costly. As a result, parcels could be sent only through the national railroad or postal service.

In fact, the shipping charge schedule revealed that it did not have to be a bad business; transporting many small packages was more profitable than transporting a large cargo, if the total weight was the same. This persuaded Masao Ogura to enter into a parcel delivery business. Were it not for his decision made against some opposition within the company, door-to-door parcel delivery service would not have been born.

3) New concept to draw customers

Yamato Transport created an innovative business of door-to-door parcel delivery service, a totally new type of transport service that did not exist in the industry. Its new business, which was named *Takkyubin*, was conceptualized as follows:

1) Collection of even a single parcel by telephone request
2) Parcel acceptance at many stores
3) Next day delivery
4) Delivery by service-minded drivers

Following the era of high economic growth in the 1960s, consumers in the 1970s were living in a prosperous society and looking for convenience in the service which they use. They were no longer satisfied with the parcel service of the national railroad, which required the sender and the recipient of a parcel to go to train stations. In response to such a need, the company started *Takkyubin* that included single parcel collection and next day delivery service. The business met the demand of the era and spread fast throughout the country.

The company's service-minded drivers made a fresh impression on customers of *Takkyubin*, since they had not expected service orientation among drivers in the transport industry. Those drivers helped improve the company's image and multiply the customers of *Takkyubin*.

4) Nationwide service network and sales drivers

Yamato Transport has an almost 50% market share in door-to-door parcel delivery service. What are their strengths that have pulled them away from their competitors?

The company's 1,800 sales offices are located throughout the country from Hokkaido to Okinawa. This nationwide service network was completed in 1997, when service began in Chichijima and Hahajima of Ogaswara (Bonin) Islands. They have also strived to multiply the stores that accept parcels for *Takkyubin*. As a result, the number of such stores has increased to about 300,000 nationwide, while *Pelikanbin*, a competing service offered by Nittsu, is handled by only 200,000 stores.

The company also benefited from its tie-in with a majority of major convenience store chains such as Seven-Eleven Japan, Lawson and FamilyMart, whose stores provide parcel acceptance service for *Takkyubin* as part of the convenience they offer to customers. This nationwide service network is the company's utmost strength that has overwhelmed its competitors.

The excellent service of *Takkyubin* is attributed not only to the hardware described above but also to the human resources. The company's drivers who collect and deliver parcels are called "sales drivers" because besides driving delivery vans, they are entrusted to find new customers and new stores to handle parcels for Yamato. Since *Takkyubin* service is used mostly by individual customers, the drivers' disposition and impression have a big impact on the sales; unfriendly drivers cannot draw customers. This is why the company has made a great effort to train service-minded drivers. The well-trained "sales drivers" are the company's strength in terms of software.

5) *Takkyubin* information system for efficiency

When a sales office of the company receives a customer's request for parcel pickup by phone, the customer's information such as the phone number and the number of parcels is stored into the computer. This information is immediately sent to a sales driver through the MCA radio system. He can see the information on a display or have it printed on a printer while staying in the vehicle he drives, and use it to arrange pickup.

The company's main sales offices are all equipped with the 4th generation *Takkyubin* information system called *Neko* system. When a sales driver calls on a customer to receive an order and collect parcels, he puts the order information on the spot into his portable POS (Point-of-Sales) terminal. The terminal prints out a label with the recipient's address, which is then attached to the parcels collected. They are now ready to go. The *Neko* system has enabled the sales drivers to finish on the spot all the paperwork for the parcels electronically. This has helped eliminate a large part of the work to be done at the main sales offices.

The sales offices are equipped with docking stations for portable POS terminals. By simply placing a portable POS terminal on the station, information stored in the terminal is automatically sent to the work station. This system eliminates the need of data transfer by drivers.

In 1998, they adopted a parcel tracking system and opened a "parcel inquiry" page linked with their home page on the Internet. The tracking system keeps track of customers' parcels and displays their whereabouts on the parcel inquiry page. The new system has helped the sales offices to reduce the number of customer service people and the time spent on the phone for answering customers' inquiries about their parcels. Thus, the *Neko* information system has been effectively used to make the *Takkyubin* system operate with great efficiency.

6) Incessant creation of new services

Because of their daily contact with customers, sales drivers have intimate knowledge of customers' needs. Such knowledge has been the source of the company's incessant creation of new services. *Cool Takkyubin, Ski Takkyubin, Golf Takkyubin, Takkyubin Time Service, Collect Service, Kuroneko Mail Service,* and *Book Service* are all value-added *Takkyubin* products. These new products can all be handled by the existing *Takkyubin* collection-delivery network and do not require new capital investment. This is the reason why the company can continue to offer new services at low cost and high quality.

In 1998, the company started *Round Trip Golf Takkyubin* jointly with its rival Nittsu. This relationship with its rival was for the convenience of customers.

Previously, many golf courses had an exclusive agreement with Nittsu for the transport of golf clubs because of the close business relationships between their parent companies and Nittsu. As a result, golfers who used Yamato's *Takkyubin* to send their golf clubs to those golf courses had to send them back home through Nittsu. In order to resolve this inconvenient arrangement for the benefit of customers, Yamato made an agreement with Nittsu to start *Round Trip Golf Takkyubin* to be shared by both parties. Golfers now have to make just one phone call for pickup, and can rest assured that their golf clubs are transported both ways. It was its commitment to *Takkyubin* service for the convenience of customers that made the company decide to cooperate with its arch rival.

7) Developing new lines of business

The company predicts that its sales will plateau someday, if it puts all its eggs in one basket of *Takkyubin*. They are therefore developing new lines of business in earnest. Their focus has been on logistics business that provides an entire range of logistical services including storage, inventory control, distributive processing, and collection of receivables. The main target of this business has been small and medium-sized companies which do not have their own logistical functions. Mail-order sales companies and others have already become the customers of this service. Yamato has accumulated business know-how of the collection of receivables through its *Collect Service*. They have also fully equipped themselves with freezing and refrigerating facilities. These know-how and facilities can be used for their logistics business. Other lines of logistical service they have developed include trunk room service and products retail business, the latter using their extensive network of parcel collection and delivery.

8) Challenging public establishment and bureaucracy —
      a spirit of defiance

The Postal Service with 24,000 post offices nationwide is the arch enemy of Yamato Transport. The birth of *Takkyubin* in 1971 inflicted a heavy blow on parcel post. Parcel post, however, staged a successful comeback after it assumed a more accessible name *Yu-Pakku* meaning postal pack(age) in 1987 and has become a strong rival of *Takkyubin*.

The Postal Service and Yamato Transport have also entered into fierce competition against each other in other services. Examples are "Registered Mail" of the Postal Service vs. "*Security Pack*" of Yamato used for the delivery of credit cards, "Chilled Yu-Pakku" vs. "*Cool Takkyubin*", and "Third-Class Mail" vs. "*Kuroneko Mail*".

The competition between the two organizations has been characterized by the superb service of Yamato met by the low price tactics of the Postal Service. Some people question the fairness of the Postal Service's tactics, because they regard offering low price regardless of the bottom line as an example of government subsidies. One thing is sure; the fierce competition between the two will continue.

Throughout its history, the company has challenged the Ministry of Transportation, which has the licensing authority over transport routes and charges. It has hewed its way through the maze of governmental bureaucracy. Its spirit of defiance has been the source of its energy.

III. Secom
Creating security system industry

(Company profile at a glance)

Financial data (Fiscal year ended March 1998)

Sales	222,541 (million yen)
Ordinary income	43,474 (million yen)
ROE	7.6%
No. of employees	11,231

Domestic market share (estimate)

Centralized security systems	60%

1) Pioneer of centralized security systems

The centralized system, the heart of Secom's security services, generates 75% of its sales revenue. Secom offers security service packages such as SECOM SX, HANKS SYSTEM, SECOM CX, and SECOM HOME SECURITY. SECOM SX puts the subscribers of the service under the remote surveillance of the control center staying on alert for emergency signals from them. HANKS SYSTEM controls the access to banks' ATM rooms and secures their safety. SECOM CX safeguards buildings. SECOM HOME SECURITY SERVICE guards the subscribers' homes against dangers such as fire, burglary, and gas leakage by putting them under 24-hour online surveillance. As many as 500,000 subscribers are safeguarded by such services.

The company also provides resident security guard service and escort service for money transport, and sells instruments for the centralized system. Its subsidiaries that belong to the Secom group are engaged in information, communication, medical and education industries.

The high earning power of the company is well demonstrated by the high ratio of ordinary income to sales, which was near 20% for the fiscal year ended March 1998. It is remarkable that the company has continued to renew its record for both sales revenue and profit in the past 35 years.

2) The advent of computer-based security system

Secom was founded in 1962 by Makoto Iida, the Director and Senior Advisor at present. It was called Nippon Keibi Hosho (Japan Security Patrols) until 1983. Initially, it was difficult to find clients and the company struggled, because security service was a new concept in society and was not, in people's mind, something to purchase from an outside vendor.

The business took off when the company was commissioned to take charge of security during the Tokyo Olympics. It also became a model for a TV program called "The Guard-Men". These events made the company famous, and its security business rapidly expanded.

Resident guard service is labor-intensive and training a large number of guards is very costly. Besides, misconduct by guards may not be avoidable. Thus, as the number of clients increased, human-based security service was reaching its limit. The company, therefore, decided

Chart 7-4   Home Security System

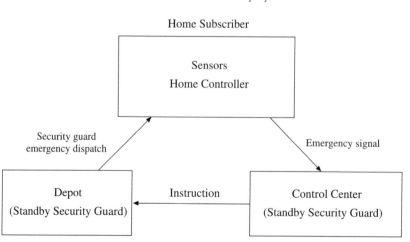

to shift its focus to a centralized system, and in 1966, it developed a machine-based surveillance system called "SP Alarm". The system also reached its limit because it still had to be monitored by human beings. This finally led to the development of the world's first computer-based security system called "CSS", in which emergency signals are received by the computer. CSS allowed the company to make a big leap forward.

The company has signed up 550,000 domestic subscribers for its service. They have also entered into markets in the US, UK, Australia, Korea, Taiwan, Malaysia, Singapore, and Indonesia. Thanks to the company's pioneering work, the new security business using a computer network has been put on a firm footing.

3) From a "safety" provider to "peace of mind" provider

The company assumed its current name Secom in 1983, when its active pursuit of diversification started. The new lines of business are all based on their core competence of computer network. One of them is the medical field.

Having been a provider of "safety", the company argued that, with "safety" secured, people would look for "peace-of-mind". The natural conclusion was to become a provider of "peace-of-mind" in the medical field. Their search for such business led them to home health care service in view of its synergy with home security service. They then acquired a US medical company to learn the know-how of the business.

Through its group companies such as Secom Care Service and Secom Home Care Service, the company is now engaged in such services as membership-based home health care, home delivery of medicine, remote imaging diagnosis for hospitals, care for the elderly, and pharmacies for Chinese medicine.

In 1998, the company started a new service to support home health care. The service permits patients at home to measure their own pulse, blood pressure, and temperature and send the data with a terminal called "Medi-data" to the care center through the telephone line. Thus, the patients can be diagnosed without doctors' visits. To participate in

Chart 7-5   Business Domain of Secom

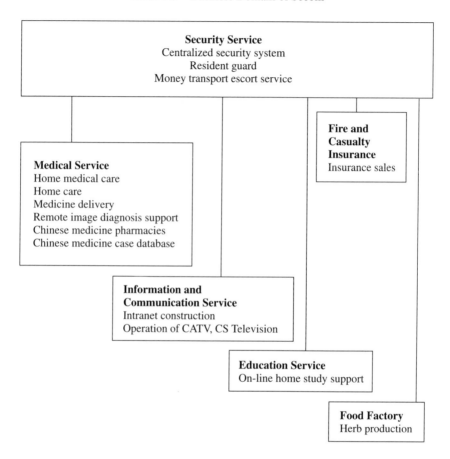

medical care service, private companies have to overcome many hurdles such as regulatory constraints and resistance of the medical association. These hurdles will test the company's competence as the pioneer of the new venture and affect the future of the business.

4) Information, communication, education, and herb production

Secom founded Secom Information System in 1991 to enter into the information-communication industry. The new company provides a service to build intranets using Secom's expertise in building security systems.

In 1995, the company founded Tokyo Internet as an Internet provider. In 1998, however, it sold the new company's entire shares to PSI, Inc. This was to concentrate its resources on network security business such as cryptograph and authentication because of its growth prospective. They also participate in the management of SKY PerfecTV and Musashi Mitaka CATV.

Secom LINES (Learning Information Network System) is the company's network service in education. The *"LINES Sensei* (= Teacher)" program has signed up about 40,000 subscribers ranging from kindergarten children to high school students.

In 1998, the company acquired Toyo Fire & Marine Insurance Co., Ltd. and entered into the fire and casualty business. This acquisition completes the plan for the new organization of the Secom group to provide the subscribers of its security service with coherent service with respect to "safety" and "peace of mind".

Secom is in the herb production business, although it is not something expected from a security service company. Twelve kinds of herbs including basil and mint are being grown in the herb plant, where light, temperature, humidity, air flow, and the concentrations of solutions are all automatically controlled. The automatic control used in the plant is based on the company's experience in the total control of buildings including the automatic control of air conditioning.

The company's core competence in security service has been used to develop new lines of business in such diversified areas as medical service, education service and herb production. The goal of its diversification is to create a "social system industry". Nearly all of their new businesses, however, have not turned profits yet. The company would be able to shed the skin and reach that goal only when the new businesses begin to turn profits.

5) Changes in management

Until recently, Secom did not have either middle-term or long-term business plans for its group companies, to which Secom functions as the holding company. For 35 years since its foundation, the Secom group was managed under the strong leadership of Makoto Iida, the founder and president of the company. He was the architect of the grand design for the Secom group to follow. His vision constituted the company's middle- and long-term plans.

In 1997, Iida resigned as the representative executive and chairman of the company, handing over the top position to Toshitaka Sugimachi. With the resignation of the charismatic leader, the company is bound to assume a new management style. Insisting on providing new products and services that had not previously existed, Iida had built Secom in its present form. How to preserve and develop this spirit of the company is a challenge presented to the new management.

6) Central control of the group personnel

Secom serves customers for their safety and peace-of-mind. How to manage its employees, therefore, is a key concern of the management. Misconduct by its employees jeopardizes the company's credibility. It is people that make the security system work, no matter how extensively it may be automated. The company, therefore, lays particular stress on the training of its employees. It has three human development centers nationwide, where nearly 10,000 employees a year receive training. Training is an indispensable vehicle to propagate Secom's ethos among its employees, many of whom have worked for other companies guided by different principles.

The basic principle of the company's human management is to reward or punish the employees according to their performance. Its reward system has been designed to motivate able workers with a variety of incentive compensation and help them grow.

The human resource management of the Secom group, which consists of 120 companies, has been centralized under the control of the head office. The head office hires people for the whole group and assign them to group companies. Human resources are actively exchanged between group companies in order to develop the abilities of employees and activate the organization. To facilitate such exchange, the group has adopted a unified wage system and a standard for job qualification and performance evaluation. Sharing of the same ethos by all the employees has become the strength of the Secom group.

Chapter Eight

Rules for Becoming a *Top Global Company*

Rule 1: Specialize in a niche

A medium-sized company can hope to make a great leap forward only when it specializes in a niche, where it can make the most of its core competence, and concentrates its resources on that niche. Niche specialization and resource concentration are the way to overcome its scale and resource limitations. *Top Global Companies* have clearly defined their business territories in which they compete.

For example, **Mabuchi Motor** has focused on small motors and fully exploited their potential, so that its products have become de facto world standards. **Yupo Corporation** has never been distracted from producing synthetic paper. These companies know that haphazard diversification causes resource diffusion and make them less competitive. *Niche specialization*, *resource concentration*, and *full exploitation of the niche* are keywords for becoming a *Top Global Company*.

Certain products and services may be a burden to big companies but a niche opportunity to a medium-sized company to become a *Top Global Company*. Examples are products made with old technology, time and labor intensive products and services, and small markets. Successful examples of companies that have taken advantage of such niche opportunities include Rohm, Nidec, and Nakashima Propeller. **Rohm** manufactures memory chips with technology a few generations old, intentionally avoiding leading-edge technology. **Nidec** specializes in low-priced, small DC motors. **Nakashima Propeller** has thrived in the small market of marine propellers. All the three companies have effectively used their flexibility to draw customers and become dominant suppliers in their respective niches. They have found niche areas where they don't have to compete with big companies.

Mabuchi Motor and other *Top Global Companies* have solid financial bases; being the price leaders in their own niches makes them highly profitable. Rich stocks of their own funds can then be invested in technology development or operations abroad to further enhance their dominance in their niche markets. Thus, specialization in a niche is the first step for a medium-sized company to becoming a *Top Global Company*.

Rule 2: Be speedy

Technical innovation is pickingup speed. Customers' needs also change very fast. In such an environment, companies have to speed up their business processes such as decision-making, product development, procurement, logistics, and marketing so that their organizations can quickly adjust themselves to changes. Thus, speed has become a prerequisite for attaining competitive advantage.

Such circumstances make characteristically slow decision-making within big companies stand out. In contrast, fast decision-making characterizes many medium-sized companies whose chief executives hold centralized power. The "go first, pull ahead" strategy works well with those companies.

Rapid change in technology takes place in the market of high speed memory testers. **Advantest** was able to dominate this market with its speedy product development. The company owes its success to its president who made a brave decision to develop next-generation memory testers ahead of its competitors.

Murata Manufacturing keeps its production processes within the company or puts them into a "black box" to prevent competitors from imitating them. By making it difficult for competitors to catch up in a short time, Murata has maintained its dominant position in the worldwide market. Companies following the "go first, pull ahead" strategy must safeguard or "black-box" proprietary technologies.

Nidec emphasizes the importance of speedy delivery when it develops prototypes. It is because they know that certain products are quickly made obsolete by fast-paced technical innovation and that spending a long time to perfect prototypes of such products does not pay off. They therefore fabricate workable prototypes in a short lead time, deliver them to customers, and use them as the basis to finalize products in cooperation with the customers. As this example of Nidec shows, speed plays the most important role in the development of high-tech products.

A successful example of speedy management in the distribution industry is **Seven-Eleven**. The company has established an information system that connects the head office, the affiliated stores and the suppliers. The system permits the stores to keep track of each of the articles sold in real-time, so that they would know exactly what to order and how many to order. The orders placed by stores are communicated on-line to suppliers and delivery centers. Finally, through the company's innovative delivery system, which was developed to facilitate frequent delivery of small batches, the ordered articles are delivered at requested time and in requested quantities. The information and delivery systems which Seven-Eleven developed minimize the time between order placement and delivery. This speedy management has made the company highly profitable.

Thus, speed can be the most powerful weapon of medium-sized companies. Finding ways to increase the speed of running their business is the road to becoming a *Top Global Company*.

Rule 3: Develop your own technology

Many of the *Top Global Companies* engineer their own production processes. Because of their quality-oriented mind-set, they do not ask vendors to do the job for them.

Mabuchi Motor, **Minebea**, **Rohm** and **Murata Manufacturing** even fabricate their own production machinery. By doing so, they can keep their proprietary technology and production know-how within the companies and prevent the information from leaking out. This allows them to maintain the technical advantages of their products for a long time and thereby avoid unwanted price-cutting competition.

Making your own production machines is far more economical than buying them from vendors. In addition, an integrated production line engineered and made by you will allow you to manufacture high quality products at low costs.

On the other hand, there are companies that achieve low cost production and core competence enhancement by not having their own fabrication facilities, namely, by being fabless. An exemplary fabless company is Keyence. **Keyence** plans for and designs products, but their manufacture is outsourced. By not having fabrication facilities, they can minimize fixed cost such as investment in facilities. Newly developed products, however, are first manufactured by their subsidiary plants so that they themselves acquire production know-how regarding those products. Later, the manufacture of those products is outsourced. Management resources concentrated on their core competence in product planning and designing permit them to strengthen it further. Thus, fabless manufacturing is an effective way for a medium-sized company to make up for the shortage of human and financial resources.

A company cannot expect to become a dominant supplier in the current global market simply by using low price as leverage. It has to have stocks of its own innovative technology and know-how that meet world standards.

Rule 4: Focus on customers

Technology-oriented companies tend to leave out customers. *Top Global Companies*, however, are all strongly customer-oriented. On the other hand, accurate prediction of the future technology trend is prerequisite to the development of best-selling products. Many of the *Top Global Companies* are eager to learn and receive hints from customers. Exemplary companies are shown below:

Tokyo Electron holds its salesmen and maintenance engineers stationed in the US responsible for collecting technical information from customers. Such information is then used to assist the company's R&D. They have built their plants near customers so that they may get wind of changes in customers' needs in time.

Rohm assigns a dedicated engineer to each customer so as to establish a close relationship with them and have full understanding of their needs. This is what has enabled the company to customize their products to the specific needs of individual customers.

Keyence's salesmen provide customers with a consulting service. Customers' needs and requests collected daily through such consulting sales are recorded on the "customer information sheet". Many hit products have been born out of the rich stock of customer information.

Advantest's sales people are always accompanied by engineers who are responsible for gathering hints from customers first-hand for new products to be developed. It is not R&D by itself but R&D tied closely with keen learning from customers that has yielded the company's best-selling products.

In the era of fierce competition, "quality" alone may not give a company a competitive advantage. Many of the *Top Global Companies*, therefore, knowingly add "service" to the quality of their products to improve customer satisfaction. This customer-oriented mind-set has made them more competitive in the marketplace.

Disco manufactures not only ultra-thin cut-off wheels but also cutting machines for using them. They advise customers on how to use the wheels and cutting machines. Thus they package together "cut-off wheels", "cutting machines", and "cutting know-how" for the convenience of customers.

Horiba has spread a maintenance service network for its emission gas analyzers throughout Europe in order to win the fierce competition there. By adding a full maintenance service to its products, Horiba has succeeded in differentiating its products from the competitors'.

As part of their consulting sales, **Keyence**'s salesmen teach customers new, effective, inexpensive ways to improve the productivity of the production lines. Such interaction with customers helps them to find new applications for their products.

All the examples described above indicate that customer focus is a key to becoming a winner in the marketplace, which is fiercely competitive now and bound to become more so in the future.

Rule 5: Expand business in a global perspective

In general, medium-sized companies enter into foreign markets first for sales, then for production, and finally for R&D. Historically, they first started offshore production in countries where low-cost labor was readily available. They then built factories in other regions to satisfy the needs of their domestic customers' plants overseas and those of overseas customers. Some of those factories were localized in order to meet regional needs.

Mabuchi Motor's division of labor on a global scale is for low cost production, and in this sense, presents a classical example of production transplant. Taking advantage of its outstanding cost-competitiveness, it has the No. 1 market share worldwide in small motors.

Denso built its overseas factories to support the global strategy of its parent company. **Tokyo Electron**'s factories are located in the vicinity of its overseas customers. This is not only to reduce logistical costs but also to respond to changes in the customers' needs in time.

Chart 8-1   Specialized Manufacturers' Entry into Overseas Markets
(Typical Pattern)

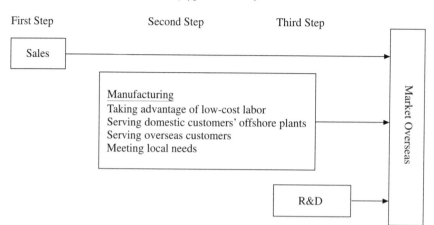

Yupo Corporation and **Nippon Electric Glass** have adapted their overseas factories to the regional needs.

While transplanting their production offshore, many companies still keep their R&D in Japan. **Minebea** is different; they moved a part of their R&D to Thailand where they manufacture. Putting production and R&D in close proximity is to encourage engineers engaged in the two functions to stimulate each other and jointly develop new technologies.

Geographical constraints are being removed by the advancement of information technology. As a result, more manufacturers will move their R&D to overseas locations where leading-edge technologies are being developed or qualified engineers are readily available.

Many companies use the domestic market as a springboard to the global market. **Horiba** and **Nidec**, however, took a reverse course of action and succeeded. In general, small, new and obscure companies in Japan face difficulty in entering the domestic market, because big companies are reluctant to take them seriously. Even if they have good products, small and medium-sized companies new in the market are not expected to become suppliers to large customers. One way for those companies to solve this dilemma is to test their products in the US market where purchase decision is made simply on the merits of the products such as quality and price. Success in the US market then becomes the gate-opener to the domestic market. This "reverse-landing" strategy helped both Horiba and Nidec. It is an effective strategy for unknown small and medium-sized companies to promote their products in the domestic market.

The borderless business world is just round the corner. A company aspiring to become a *Top Global Company*, therefore, has to be capable of expanding its business in a global perspective.

Rule 6: Use information technology to your advantage

Remarkable progress has been made in information technology. *Top Global Companies* are keenly aware of this and take full advantage of it for saving labor and improving customer service.

For example, **Denso** is working on the construction of an online network in which physical "Kanban" or order instruction cards are replaced with electronic Kanban. Once completed, the network will connect all the parts manufacturers within the Toyota group and greatly reduce the lead time between order placement and delivery.

CAD has allowed **Nakashima Propeller** to reduce the time for designing a propeller from about 10 days to only 5 minutes.

Tokyo Electron is working on a service network to provide customers with on-line manuals for trouble shooting and repair. Once completed, the network will enable customers to perform maintenance work by themselves by following the manual displayed on the computer screen, and as a result, make up for the shortage of maintenance personnel.

Horiba has online a new web page in which information of a new product under development is disclosed. On that page, customers can present their opinions on the product. This joint product development with customers is to facilitate the integration of customers' needs into new products.

It is their information system more than anything else that has enabled **Seven-Eleven**, **Yamato Transport** and **Secom** to expand the new businesses they created:

Seven-Eleven is equipped with a multimedia information system that consists of subsystems such as the "POS Information System", "Store System", and "Order, Logistics and Clients System". The POS information collected in real time not only helps stores to improve the accuracy of their order placement, but also facilitates product development.

An increasing number of customers pay their public utility bills at **Seven-Eleven** stores. Were it not for the information system, Seven-Eleven would not have been able to offer this type of service. The information system is also used to transmit instructions and sales promotion material quickly from the head office to the affiliated stores. It has become an indispensable tool for every division of the company.

All of the delivery vans of **Yamato Transport** are connected with sales offices through the MCA radio system, so that the orders received by sales offices are transmitted to the sales drivers of delivery vans. The company's main sales offices are equipped with 4th generation *Neko* system that permits the sales drivers to enter a customer's order information into a portable terminal on the spot. Thus, the information technology helps make parcel pickup and delivery more efficient and reduce administrative work for the main sales offices. Furthermore, the company has a "parcel inquiry" web page that allows customers to keep track of their parcels.

Secom runs its centralized security business through a computer network that connects 500,000 or more subscribers of their service, 47 control centers, and 850 depots around the country. According to an estimate, a manned security system of a similar scale would require more than one million people, which indicates huge labor saving by the computer network. In addition, the company's new lines of business such as a medical service and home shopping service rely on the computer network.

While it requires a considerable investment to construct, an information system can supplement limited human resources. Thus, the effective use of information technology can make up for the scale disadvantage of medium-sized companies and enable them to compete against big companies on an equal footing.

Rule 7: Initiate personnel management to boost workers' morale

A medium-sized company has only a limited stock of human resources. The morale of each of its employees, therefore, has a profound impact on its health. In view of this, *Top Global Companies* have adopted human resource management systems that boost employees' morale and support energetic organizations.

Many of the *Top Global Companies* have adopted merit-based reward systems that directly link achievement with monetary reward. For example, both **Nidec** and **Rohm** have award systems in which employees who have accomplished outstanding achievements are recognized with honor and cash prizes, the highest of which is 10 million yen in both systems. It is probably safe to say that those award systems involving big cash prizes are accepted only because the two companies are medium-sized; rewarding workers for their achievements with cash, let alone a large amount, is a concept rather foreign to big companies in Japan.

Almost all the *Top Global Companies* link the performance and ability of employees with their salary and promotion. For example, both **Rohm** and **Keyence** disclose the performance of each of their divisions to boost competitive spirit among their employees. **Murata Manufacturing** requires each of the management units to strictly manage its costs and each of its employees to be conscious of the profit and loss of his or her division.

Keyence has adopted a shrewd performance-based reward system, which lets only capable workers survive. This fierce competition for survival has created an energetic organization. As early as in 1966,

Rohm's staff began to receive salary on an annual basis; lifetime employment is not a rule at Rohm.

Some companies believe that strict control is not the only way to improve the quality and efficiency of the work to be performed, but that letting workers work on what they take interest in is the key to that goal. For example, **Horiba** defines the workplace as the place for self-realization, and has offered a proper working environment where workers can develop their own individuality. On the other hand, the company requires that its employees be able to do what others cannot do, and if they are unable to fulfill this then they have to leave. **Denso** has started an open recruiting system, in which its employees can apply for job offers in new lines of business. It also opened the way for a switch from a general clerical job to a main career track. These new systems are aimed at activating the organization through personnel exchange. **Nidec** also uses an open recruiting system within the company to give a chance to motivated, able workers. **Murata Manufacturing** uses the "principal job system" to train its employees to become career-long specialists in their "principal jobs". Being able to choose their own specialization, the company's employees can focus on their jobs at hand.

Some companies delegate the authorization power of the top management in order to achieve speedy management and enhance the sense of responsibility within the organization. For example, **Murata Manufacturing** has authorized the general manager of each division to approve capital investment of 2 billion yen or less. This is to enhance the sense of responsibility of each division for its own profit and loss and promotes speedy decision-making throughout the company. At **Advantest,** the delegation of the top management's authority has raised the sense of participation among its employees and enhanced speedy management.

In order to facilitate personnel exchange within the group, **Secom** and **Murata Manufacturing** use unified standards for wage, job qualification, and performance evaluation for the head office and the subsidiaries. Being treated on the same footing no matter where they work, their employees are highly motivated.

Thus, a medium-sized company aspiring to become a dominant supplier in the global market has to initiate a personnel management system that boosts the morale of its limited human resource.

Chapter Nine

People and Organization of
Top Global Companies

I. Leaders of *Top Global Companies*

The leaders of *Top Global Companies*, the founders in particular, have powerful personalities, which are reflected in the technology, products and management systems of those companies. Although they lead their companies in their own distinctive fashions, they have some characteristics in common that distinguish them as the leaders in the global market. Those are as follows:

- ♦ Clear-cut managerial principles
- ♦ Sharing of the managerial principles by all the employees
- ♦ Focus that determines the business domain
- ♦ Great foresight and the ability to get things done
- ♦ Ambitious goals
- ♦ Out-of-the-box thinking
- ♦ Widely spread network for collecting information

1) Clear-cut managerial principles

The dreams and convictions of the leader of a company are condensed in the company's managerial principle. The leader of a *Top Global Company* articulates his managerial principle and directs his company accordingly. It is this principle that lets the employees cherish a dream and urges them to work toward its achievement.

For a company that ventures into an untrodden field of business, the managerial principle of the leader is the only guide and therefore the basis for the company's code of conduct and code of ethics. It is embodied in the company's vision, code of conduct, mission statement, motto and operating policy.

Secom conducts its business according to the ten articles that comprise *"Secom's Principle"*. Its diversification into medical, education, information and communication services follows its principle of making society a safe place to live.

Advantest's mission is to *"support at the leading edge the latest technology embodied in semiconductors"*. The convergence of the whole energy of the company in this mission enabled Advantest to be the first in the world to develop the fastest semiconductor tester.

Disco's mission is to *"deliver satisfaction in substance to customers"*. When they developed an ultra-thin cut-off wheel, customers could not use it because no cutting machines suitable for the wheel were available on the market. They therefore developed their own cutting machine and marketed it with the ultra-thin cut-off wheel. Since then, it has become their strategy to *"deliver satisfaction in substance to customers by providing them with abrasive wheels, cutting machines and application technology"*. This strategy substantiates the company's mission.

A clear-cut managerial principle helps motivate employees and direct them toward a common goal. To the leader of a company, articulating the company's managerial principle assumes utmost importance.

2) Sharing of the managerial principle by all employees

Unless shared by all the employees, the managerial principle of a company has no value. For this reason, *Top Global Companies* have strived to propagate their principles throughout the organization.

Mabuchi Motor manufactures 100% of its products at offshore factories. Its motto is *"Co-existence and Co-prosperity in Adopted*

Countries". They know that they cannot co-exist and co-prosper with people in the countries they have adopted, if they move their factories at will to wherever cheaper labor is available. As one country's economy advances, therefore, instead of uprooting the factory located there, they upgrade its technology so that it can perform more sophisticated work. Thus, they have substantiated their motto by nurturing long-term relationships with the countries where they have built factories.

Minebea emphasizes the importance of *"hands-on training on the shop floor"*. Engineers of Minebea factories learn how to assemble new production machines which they use. Through this hands-on training, the engineers gain in-depth knowledge of those machines and acquire the advanced skill to operate them. The company's idea of learning skills through *"hands-on training on the shop floor"* has been well understood by all the employees.

Keyence's motto is *"Maximum profits with minimum capital"*. According to this principle, the company has adopted fabless production, minimizing the fixed cost (capital investment, maintenance cost, etc.). As a result, it has become a highly profitable company, with the ratio of operating income to sales exceeding 40%.

3) Focus that determines the business domain

The leaders of *Top Global Companies* are focused on distinct markets, products or technologies. Take Rohm for instance. Custom ICs have been **Rohm**'s focus. The company has effectively used its flexibility as leverage against big companies which are reluctant to entertain time-consuming custom ICs. Rohm's business domain has been carved out by its focus on custom ICs, which are developed in close cooperation with customers. On the other hand, being focused on small motors and propellers for large ships, respectively, **Mabuchi Motor** and **Nakashima Propeller** have thoroughly explored pertinent technology and developed their own proprietary technical know-how. It is their scrupulous pursuit of technology that has made them the world's no. 1 companies in their specialties. These three examples show how the focus of each leader of a *Top Global Company* has determined their business domain.

4) Great foresight and the ability to get things done

Top Global Companies owe their current positions to the great foresight and intuition of their founders who could perceive the future of unprecedented enterprises. Having found business to focus on, these founders cherished a dream and a desire. They, however, knew that their dream would never be realized without the very first step, which they took.

The leaders of *Top Global Companies* have the ability to take key steps to move their companies forward. They take the lead in getting things done, which energizes the company and guides it toward success. Thus, they lead their companies with their great foresight and ability to get things done.

Shigenobu Nagamori, the founder of **Nidec**, was quick to perceive the great future of small DC motors. His target was to make his company the world's no. 1 supplier of DC motors. He worked non-stop all year round. He built an energetic organization, with all the employees indoctrinated with the three company mottos: "Passion, zeal, persistence", "Work hard, use the mind", and "Act immediately, do without fail, work to complete". His foresight and ability to get things done led to the realization of the dream he had cherished.

5) Ambitious goals

The leaders of *Top Global Companies* set the goals for their companies so high that they sometimes seem unachievable. If the dream of the leader of a company is also cherished by the employees, however, a very ambitious goal can induce at all levels within the organization "strategic intent" to close the gap between the target and reality. A larger gap is expected to make the employees more motivated to create strategies to make a leap. Strategies to "Make the impossible possible" or

"Enable the lesser to win against the greater" are then born to meet a tough challenge. This is the reason why the leaders of *Top Global Companies* set extremely high goals for their companies. Take **Nidec** for example. The sales of Nidec proper grew to 100 billion yen in only 25 years after the company was founded. The company aims to increase the sales of the Nidec group to 1 trillion yen by the year 2010. Preaching that the growth (of the business) is driven by and promised to adventurous spirits, the president, Mr. Nagamori, attempts to boost the energy of the company.

6) Out-of-the-box thinking

Successful companies have a general tendency to retire into their own shells. On the contrary, the leaders of *Top Global Companies* have opened up new avenues of their own by thinking out of the box as shown by the following examples:

Ogura Masao, former president of **Yamato Transport**, predicted that the demand for parcel delivery services would grow as consumers become more prosperous. The idea prevalent in the transport industry at that time was that money couldn't be made on a parcel delivery service. Against the opposition around him, however, he entered into a door-to-door parcel delivery service. With its consumer-oriented service such as a pickup service even for a single parcel and next day delivery, the new service named *Takkyubin* quickly expanded its market. This new business was the brainchild of the leader who questioned the conventional wisdom of the industry.

Yupo Corporation developed outdoor posters and food labels markets for the synthetic paper by taking advantage of its characteristics such as water resistance, tear resistance and printability. Being hard to fold is a defect in the applications where the synthetic paper is expected to behave like paper. The company, however, promoted the hard-to-fold synthetic paper as an easy-to-unfold paper and succeeded in selling it for ballots. It is the company's flexible thinking that has helped find applications for the synthetic paper.

7) Widely spread network for collecting information

The leaders of *Top Global Companies* have a sharp sense of finding out information. They are quick to get wind of business opportunities as the following examples show.

Convenience stores, which are part of our daily lives now, were not invented in Japan. In the 1970s, a law was enacted to protect small and medium-sized retailers by putting restrictions on large stores in the shopping districts. In order to overcome this difficulty, Toshifumi Suzuki, president of Ito-Yokado, contemplated opening small stores in those restricted shopping areas. Then through the network he had built he came across Seven-Eleven (U.S.A.), and **Seven-Eleven Japan** was born. Thanks to his sensitivity to not only domestic but also overseas information, the chain of convenience stores was transplanted to Japan and blossomed.

In 1961, Makoto Iida, founder of **Secom**, heard from a friend about the existence of security service companies in Europe. This inspired him to start the first security business in Japan.

As the above examples show, the leaders of *Top Global Companies* spread their networks, always searching for hints for business opportunities.

II. Management Style in the Era of Globalization

1) Changes in the management style caused by globalization

Globalization of the economy is changing the way Japanese companies are organized and managed. Businesses becoming borderless, those rules which are valid in Japan but cannot be accepted by other countries have to change. Japanese companies have to reform the management systems they have been used to for a long time. Even Sony, which has been viewed as the most global company in Japan, had to reform its board of directors in order to enhance corporate governance according to the global standard. Standing at this critical juncture, what are the leaders of Japanese companies planning to reform and how?

According to the "Questionnaire to 100 Presidents of Companies", which was conducted by the *Nihon Keizai Shimbun* in April 1998, many presidents said they should reform their "top management", "board of directors", and "attitude toward shareholders". They are aware that they will not be able to survive the era of globalization if they continue to follow the traditional decision-making process or management system that pays little attention to shareholders. They are even going to change the basic systems that have supported the growth of the Japanese economy, namely, the "horizontalism", which has restricted competition in the industry, and the traditional wage system and employment pattern.

Chart 9-1   Japanese Company's Most Important Reformation Targets
for Their Self Renewal

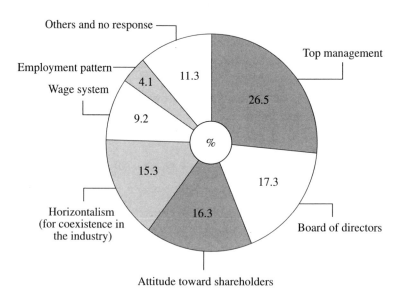

(Source: Nikkei Sangyo Shimbun, 22 April 1998)

In the process of casting off the old skin of Japanese style management, the leaders of Japanese companies are searching for new management styles that meet global standards. New management systems that have been adopted for that purpose include the ROE-based management, slim board of directors, merit-based human resource management, and performance-linked dividend policy.

Many of the *Top Global Companies* have already been managed in styles close to the world standards. This is partially due to their long experience in export and offshore manufacturing. Having won competition in the borderless market, these companies present models for other Japanese companies to follow.

2) Reformation of the board of directors in progress

In 1997, Sony drastically reduced the number of board members from 38 to 10. The new board decides on the strategic plans for Sony's headquarters and group companies, while "execution executives" are entrusted to execute the plans for each division. The slim board and the separation of decision-making on the strategic plans from the execution of the plans are expected to accelerate company-wide decision-making.

The new board that oversees the company management consists of three external and seven internal directors, which makes corporate governance highly transparent. Sony consciously reformed its board according to global standard, although the ratio of external directors to internal ones is lower than that in American corporations. This reformation has made a strong impact on other Japanese companies.

Many *Top Global Companies* perform speedy management with a slim board of directors. Keyence, Rohm, and Horiba have only 5, 6, and 7 directors, respectively. These numbers are much smaller than 15.03 (Toyo Keizai 1996), the average number of directors of the listed companies.

Kenichiro Sato, president of Rohm, says that his company's six directors can get together and make decisions over lunch every day. In contrast to the speedy decision-making of *Top Global Companies* under the strong leadership of their leaders, that of big companies takes time, because they generally follow a bottom-up decision-making process. Thus, the difference in the organization and function of the board of directors is reflected in the difference in the speed of decision-making between *Top Global Companies* and big companies.

3) Reforming Japanese style employment system

Increasingly, fierce competition in the global market and the aging of the population force companies in Japan to reform their employment systems. The Japanese style employment system, which is characterized by lifetime employment and seniority-based wage, functioned effectively in the era of high economic growth. Its shortcomings, however, have become more apparent in recent years. As a result, companies in Japan have begun to adopt ability- and performance-based human resource management systems, which include ability-based wage plans, annual salary systems, and specialist systems.

Merit-based personnel management is nothing new to *Top Global Companies*. It is a policy they have adopted not to conform to the global standard, but rather to make the most of their limited human resources so as to "enable the lesser to win against the greater". It has helped them to boost competitive spirit among the employees and maintain the vitality of the organizations. Human power is the source of the competitive power of *Top Global Companies*.

Rohm rejected lifetime employment, and in 1966 adopted an annual salary system for general managers and those above. The ability-based portion of their salary, which amounts to 50% of the total, is determined by performance review. Competent managers can be promoted to directors in their 40s. The company strictly adheres to the policy of rewarding or punishing the employees according to their performance. In 1990, for example, half of the board members were fired, bearing the blame for the poor performance of the company.

Under the shrewd achievement-based reward system of **Keyence**, the retention rate of its sales force is extremely low. The company, however, does not consider the low retention rate negative, for it believes that the mobile work force activates the organization. The human resource management of Rohm and Keyence is opposite to that of big companies whose focus is on the retention of their large work force.

Denso is attempting to reform its corporate culture as a means to strengthen the company against fierce competition. A performance-based personnel evaluation system has been introduced to boost competitive spirit among the employees.

Murata has used the "principal job" system to nurture its employees into becoming experts of their principal jobs. This is to use the human resource's quality as a means to make up for a lack of quantity.

Companies that have grown rapidly supplement their lack of human resource by recruiting or headhunting people who have worked for other companies before. In order to create an innovative atmosphere, many companies deliberately mix those people with old employees who have worked for them from the beginning of their career. Innovations are hard to come by in the organization of a big company and from its people who are cultivated in the unmixed culture of the company. The innovativeness of *Top Global Companies* is a result of the interaction among people from different backgrounds.

Shigenobu Nagamori, president of **Nidec**, spends much time headhunting. He also actively pursues M&A to procure an entire package of an external organization and its people. The interaction among people cultivated in different cultures creates energy, which supports the rapid growth of the company.

The human resource management of *Top Global Companies* is far more progressive than that of big companies and relevant in this era of globalization. Those big companies which cannot reform their Japanese style employment systems are sure to be left behind.

4) Managing companies according to international
   accounting standards

The global standardization of accounting practices is imminent. Many of the *Top Global Companies* are preparing for the adoption of the International Accounting Standards based on current value accounting and consolidated accounting as the following examples show:

Denso has decided to use a new financial system based on consolidated accounting. Once the new system starts in year 2000, the company's offshore subsidiaries will be forced to focus on profit.

The global standardization has also affected the distribution of dividends; an increasing number of companies have adopted performance-linked dividend policies in place of stable dividend policies.

Horiba was fast to link dividends for a fiscal year with the profit and loss of that period rather than distribute dividends as a percentage of par value. Hardly any objection was raised when **Tokyo Electron** announced that, from the fiscal year ending in March 1999 onward, it would distribute performance-linked dividends in place of stable dividends. It was because a majority of shareholders preferred an increase in the stock price to stable dividends. Foreign investors, who own a large percentage of the shares of the two companies, have favored their dividend policies that conform to global standards.

There are many *Top Global Companies* that have taken positive steps towards information disclosure. **Rohm** and **Murata** disclose their financial information on the Internet. For investors' convenience, **Horiba** has published pamphlets that contain their consolidated financial statements and other financial information. Information disclosure by a company has the positive effect of drawing investors' interest to its stock, which results in higher stock prices. In this regard, investor relations will play an increasingly important role in the management of companies.

In America, ROE (Return on Equity) is considered a key business index. The average ROE of American companies (those included in the calculation of S&P Composite Index of 500 Stocks) was 20.8% in 1997, while that of Japanese companies (those included in the calculation of Nikkei Average Stock Index, financial institutions excluded) was only 2.9% (source: Yamato Soken). This low capital efficiency of Japanese companies is due to their preoccupation with sales and market share.

Many *Top Global Companies* place more emphasis on the organization's efficiency than its expansion, which results in a high ROE. As the market becomes more conscious of the concept of a "company that is for its shareholders", the management policy that has driven *Top Global Companies* to achieve high ROE is in the spotlight.

5) Social responsibility in the era of globalization

It has been argued that Japanese companies have been managed with little transparency and lack a strong sense of social responsibility. The situation is changing. Progress in globalization forces Japanese companies to fulfill such social responsibility as accepted in the international community. They must establish corporate governance that ensures their strict adherence to public laws and regulations. They must be run by ethical and conscientious management. They are expected to contribute not only to the local communities but also to the global society.

Many of the *Top Global Companies* strive to fulfill their social responsibility with a global perspective. **Rohm**, for example, is committed to ridding its production lines of all the chemicals that destroy the ozone layer and recycle the industrial waste generated by its factories. **Horiba** also places utmost importance on the preservation of the global environment.

An increasing number of companies in Europe and America require their suppliers to be certified by ISO 14001, the international standards for environmental control. *Top Global Companies* are conscious of this, because a majority of their export customers are located in those regions. It is clear that the global market is not going to accept companies that are ignorant of environmental issues.

Some of the *Top Global Companies* are active in contributing to the local communities and supporting cultural activities. Contribution to the society by a company is not only the expression of the company leader's ethics and virtue but also an issue important to the very existence of the company. Companies just seeking for profits are opposed by the society, which makes it difficult to recruit able people. The morale of the employees of *Top Global Companies* is high, because they are proud to be working for companies that contribute to the society.

Rohm generously supports the arts. Having aspired to be a pianist when he was young, Kenichiro Sato, president of the company, is well versed in music. Through the Rohm Music Foundation, the company has been supporting a wide range of music activities. It has also contributed to the community of Kyoto, where it is located, by publishing the city's cultural history and supporting traditional performing arts.

As a director of the Venture Enterprise Center, an incorporated foundation, and a director of the Sanwa Venture Fostering Fund, Masao Horiba, the founder of **Horiba**, helps venture businesses to grow.

Mabuchi Motor's motto "Coexistence and Co-prosperity in Adopted Countries" represents the corporate spirit to follow in the era of globalization.

Concluding Remarks

The Japanese-style management was once in the spotlight on the world stage. Lifetime employment, seniority-based wage system, cooperative labor-management relationship, close relationships among the government, bureaucracy and industry, and business affiliations, called *Keiretsu*, were all considered the source of Japan's strengths. Some even argued that the Japanese-style business organization was the mother of innovation.

The situation has changed. Since the latter half of the 1990s, large and supposedly strong corporations have gone under one after another. Praise for Japanese-style management has subsided, and Japanese companies have begun to be referred to as examples of losers.

Market economy, however, does not make all the companies losers. As long as the market functions, there are always winners achieving high profits. Among those winners are *Top Global Companies* that have a top worldwide market share in their specialties. They have long been focused on specific niches, improved the speed of their business undertaking, and effectively used information technology. The authors set out to study those companies and analyze their practices so as to gain insight into the way companies should be managed in the 21st century.

Globalization has forced many business leaders to grope for post Japanese-style management. They are paying more attention to "efficiency versus expansion", "specialization versus integration", and "profit versus employment". Thus, new management styles they are to follow are coming infinitely closer to the management style of *Top Global*

Companies. Mere imitation of the management style, however, would not permit companies to shed the old skin to become strong companies. Many leaders of *Top Global Companies* have strong personalities. They have been intensely focused on certain technologies and markets. Their philosophies and convictions have led their companies to establish de facto standards for the technology in their specialties. Entrepreneurial spirits run in the veins of those companies.

Through the writing of the present book, the authors renewed their conviction that entrepreneurship is indispensable to the revitalization of the Japanese industry. It is our sincere wish that many new *Top Global Companies* will be born for the revitalization of the Japanese economy.

And last but not least, we would like to express our heart-felt thanks to Mr. Masatoshi Kasuya, chief editor of Sanno College Publishing Department, for his unfailing support.

Tokyo   Akira Ishikawa
March 3, 1999   Tai Nejo

Bibliography

Books (written in Japanese)

Akiba, Yoshinobu, ed. *Iida Akira Carries Through His Purpose.* Toyo Keizai Inc., 1998.

Asano, Noriyuki. *Secrets of Small Companies Having No. 1 Market Shares in Japan.* Kou Shobo, 1995.

Diamond Inc.'s Company Exploration Team, ed. *The Way a Company Evolves — Keyence.* Diamond Inc., 1996.

Economic Planning Agency, ed. *Japan's Economy White paper 1998.* Ministry of Finance Printing Bureau, 1998.

Fukushima, Yoshiaki. *Revolution in Supply Chain Management.* Nihon Keizai Shimbun, Inc., 1998.

Horiba, Masao. *Masao Horiba Talks about Management.* Toyo Keizai Inc., 1998.

Ishikawa, Akira, and Nejo, Tai. *Why Seven-Eleven is the Sole Winner.* Sanno Institute of Management Publication Department, 1998.

Ishikawa, Akira. *Introduction to Strategic Information System*, Rev. ed. Nihon Keizai Shimbun, Inc., 1997.

Itami, Takayuki, et al. *Case Book: Managerial Behavior of Japanese Companies — 2, Entrepreneurship and Strategy.* Yuhikaku, 1998.

_____. *Case Book: Managerial Behavior of Japanese Companies — 3, Innovation and Technology.* Yuhikaku, 1998.

Karatsu, Hajime. *Japan — the Sun Will Rise.* PHP Institute, 1998.

_____. *Sellable Products Sell.* PHP Institute, 1998.

Keizaiki "Pocket History" Editorial Committee, ed. *Nidec*. Keizaikai, 1997.

Konno, Noboru, and Ikujiro Nonaka. *Intellectual Management*. Nihon Keizai Shimbun, Inc., 1996.

Kunitomo, Ryuichi. *Information Revolution by Seven-Eleven*. Pal Publishing, 1993.

Makino, Noboru. *Resilient Strength of Japan's Technology*. PHP Institute, 1998.

Matsuoka, Isao. *Study of New Company Groups — NEC Group*. Nippon Jitsugyo Publishing, 1996.

Ministry of International Trade and Industry, ed. *International Trade White Paper (Outline) 1998*. Ministry of Finance Printing Bureau, 1998.

Mizushima, Atsuo. *Strategic Business Platform*. Diamond Inc., 1998.

Nagamori, Shigenobu. *Be a Leader to Motivate People*. Mikasa Shobo, 1998.

Nikkei Business, ed. *Source of the Strength of the Company*. Nikkei BP, 1997.

Ogata, Tomoyuki. *Information Revolution in Distribution by Seven-Eleven — Ito Yokada*. TBS Britannica, 1995.

Ozawa, Yukimasa, Koji Sakamoto, and Takashi Tezuka, ed. *Small World No. 1 Companies*. Doyukan, 1997.

Tatezawa, Koji. *Super Distribution Revolution by Yamato Transport*. OS Publishing, 1997.

Watanabe, Yoshihiko. *Innovative Management of Companies Having Top Market Shares*. Hakuto Shobo, 1998.

Books (translated into Japanese)

Goldman, Steven L., et al. *Agile Competition* (translation of the original "*Agile Competitors and Virtual Organizations*" in English). Nihon Keizai Shimbun, Inc., 1996.

Hammel, G., and C. K. Prahalad. *Core Competence Management* (translation of the original "*The Core Competence of the Corporation*" in English). Nihon Keizai Shimbun, Inc., 1995.

Porter, M. E. *Strategy of Competitive Advantage* (translation of the original "*Competitive Advantage*" in English). Diamond Inc., 1996.

Journals (in Japanese)

Weekly Diamond, 5 July 1997, Diamond Inc.

Weekly Toyo Keizai, 12 December 1998, Toyo Keizai Inc.

Nikkei Business, 12 June 1995, Nikkei BP.

Nikkei Business, 2 October 1995, Nikkei BP.

Nikkei Business, 3 June 1996, Nikkei BP.

Nikkei Business, 30 June 1997, Nikkei BP.

Nikkei Business, 6 October 1997, Nikkei BP.

Nikkei Business, 11 May 1998, Nikkei BP.

Nikkei Business, 24 August 1998, Nikkei BP.

Nikkei Business, 6 October 1998, Nikkei BP.

Nikkei Information Strategy, January 1998, Nikkei BP.

Zaikai, extra number, 10 January 1999, Zaikai Institute.

The 21, May 1998, PHP Institute.

Financial Statements (in Japanese)

Advantest Comprehensive Financial Statements, March 1998.

Canon Kasei Sales Report (1997 January 1–1997 December 31).

Denso Comprehensive Financial Statements, March 1998.

Horiba Comprehensive Financial Statements, March 1998.

Keyence Comprehensive Financial Statements, March 1998.

Mabuchi Motor Comprehensive Financial Statements, December 1997.

Minebea Comprehensive Financial Statements, March 1998.

Murata Manufacturing Comprehensive Financial Statements, March 1998.

Nihon Electric Glass Comprehensive Financial Statements, March 1998.

Rohm Comprehensive Financial Statements, March 1998.

Secom Comprehensive Financial Statements, March 1998.

Seven-Eleven Japan Comprehensive Financial Statements, February 1998.

Tokyo Electron Comprehensive Financial Statements, March 1998.

Yamato Transport Comprehensive Financial Statements, March 1998.

Databases (in Japanese)

Rohm Brochure (1997)

Nikkei Company Information, 1998 summer edition (1998).

Kaisha Shikiho — Unlisted Companies, 1999 first half edition (1998).

Nikkei Management Indexes of Listed Companies, 1998 fall (1998).

Nikkei Management Indexes of Unlisted, Over-the-Counter Companies, 1999 (1998).

Newspapers (in Japanese)

Nihon Keizai Shimbun

Nikkei Sangyo Shimbun

Nikkei Ryutsu Shimbun

Nikkei Kin'yu Shimbun

Nikkan Kogyo Shimbun

Index

M